THE WOUNDED HEART

A Companion Workbook for Personal or Group Use

Dr. Dan B. Allender

NAVPRESS ●

BRINGING TRUTH TO LIFE

P.O.BOX 35001, COLORADO SPRINGS, COLORADO 80935

The Navigators is an international Christian organization.
Our mission is to reach, disciple, and equip people to
know Christ and to make him known through successive
generations. We envision multitudes of diverse people in
the United States and every other nation who have a
passionate love for Christ, live a lifestyle of sharing
Christ's love, and multiply spiritual laborers among those
without Christ.

NavPress is the publishing ministry of The Navigators.
NavPress publications help believers learn biblical truth
and apply what they learn to their lives and ministries.
Our mission is to stimulate spiritual formation among our
readers.

© 1992 by Dan B. Allender
Revised edition © 1995
All rights reserved. With the exception of pages 143-144
    as specified on page 142, no part of this publication
    may be reproduced in any form without written
    permission from NavPress, P.O. Box 35001, Colorado
    Springs, CO 80935.
ISBN 08910-96655

Printed in the United States of America

5 6 7 8 9 10 11 12 13 14 15 / 99

CONTENTS

Preface   **7**

ONE
Getting Started   **11**

TWO
Secondary Symptoms   **23**

THREE
Facing the Battle   **31**

FOUR
Stages of Abuse   **43**

FIVE
Shame   **55**

SIX
Contempt   **67**

SEVEN
Powerlessness   **83**

EIGHT
Ambivalence   **107**

NINE
Betrayal   **125**

TEN
Style of Relating   **137**

ELEVEN
Repentance   **153**

TWELVE
Bold Love   **165**

A Note to Group Members   **181**

Ideas for Group Leaders   **183**

*To those who have the hunger and courage
to seek God.*

PREFACE

One woman described the process of dealing with her abuse as a cure that at times seemed worse than the disease. The process of change is rarely easy; the decisions at important forks in the road are not quickly clear. Why would anyone choose to proceed on such a difficult journey? The truest answer—for the sake of the glory of God—assumes a more godly motivation than most abuse victims are ready to acknowledge.

The most readily offered answer for why someone might purchase this workbook and pursue change is the ache of unhappiness. We all desire a more stable, tranquil inner world and a less abusive, conflictive, and painful world of relationships. We want a better world. Any guide, be it book or person, that seems to offer a path to happiness will sell, but it might not really help—that is, help the pilgrim gain perspective and strength to journey to a far better end than mere happiness. If the motivation to pursue the difficult path is simply personal unhappiness, then the journey will become trapped in its own self-oriented vicious circle.

Let me try to explain. A woman I counseled put words to this dilemma when it became apparent that her growth was beginning to disrupt her disengaged husband: "I am alive in ways I never dreamed possible, but I am finding reality is more of a nightmare than it was when I lived in the deluded, distorted fog of self-hatred. I pursued counseling in order to find healing; and the change I've experienced has taken me into new regions of joy. But it has also opened more wounds, exposed more sins than I imagined, and propelled me into new struggles with people I used to get along with fine. What's wrong with me?"

What she perceived to be the problem was in fact the fruit of repentant brokenness and the flowering change of new resurrected beauty. Her change, in certain ways, deepened her joy, strength, and passion. The change was lovely, but it was also highly threatening to her husband and friends. And that disruption of the status quo violated the main reason she came for counseling. She never felt as if she fit in any group or was enjoyed in any relationship. She wanted to be happy; and she came to counseling to be healed, free, alive. But the fruit of healing, freedom, and aliveness is not always happiness. Biblical change actually opens a new realm of service and worship that, at times, puts one at odds with relationships that were founded on our willingness to be sick, enslaved, and dead. If personal happiness is the sole reason you are considering this workbook, I believe you will be disappointed.

My client struggled with this question: "Why choose change?" Her increased aliveness led to new conflicts. She often handled the new struggles by growing detached and hard; she kept her growing joy imprisoned behind strong boundaries of independence and anger; and her beauty wilted in the ultraviolet light of self-centeredness. She seemed trapped. Change brought conflict; conflict intensified the desire to succumb to the old patterns. She was caught on the horns of both desiring deeper change and understanding what change requires.

The vicious cycle can be broken only when a deeper impetus for change joins the legitimate desire for happiness. Let me say it again. The desire to be happy is the reason all of us began our return to the Father. There is something honorable about recognizing our current status in the pigpen as dishonorable and beneath our dignity (Luke 15:14-20). Change, true biblical healing, occurs when we are wholly dissatisfied with our condition of heart and soul. But more is required than merely the legitimate desire for happiness; we must comprehend that our deepest happiness will be found only in relationship with our Father. And relationship with Him is found through what appears to be the utter loss of our agenda (happiness) and the pursuit of His agenda (His own glory). At first it sounds like a soul-destroying return to the experience of the past abuse: give up your soul for the sake of someone else's pleasure. Therefore, the central issue I hope to help you ponder is your relationship with God. Where was He when you were abused? Is He good? Is He trustworthy; and if so, what can you ask of Him?

A core question must be asked: Is God like our abusers? What He seems to require—trust, brokenness, and love on His terms—feels like the requirements of an abuser. Or is our perception of God so confused by past abuse that it is difficult to know who He is? I believe the evil one cleverly has tried to mirror in the stages of abuse God's relationship with us, so that intimacy, trust, pleasure, and desire would always seem tainted by the horrendous betrayal of abuse. I believe God is trustworthy and good, but the fact that I believe that will not help you until you have wrestled with God to discover His goodness and mercy.

I've come to realize that the only valid and lasting reason to change is to know God, to embrace His purposes for my life and to deepen my loving anticipation in His coming. In Him, and only in Him, is happiness to be found. But don't for a minute read these words as an ascetic denial of or a pious discouragement against human pleasure. A pursuit of God's glory is the only route for comprehending the deepest possible human pleasure. True hedonism and true humanism are available only to those who know the One who made all pleasure and who chose to become human Himself.

The reason to pursue change is so that I can look at a sunset, read a novel, hold my daughters or son, drink deep from a friendship, sit quietly in prayer, or ponder heaven and simultaneously weep, laugh, and marvel. I want to know God, to experience what it means to be alive in His presence, then return to Him the praise of my grateful heart. If that is your desire—even if it is small and other motives apparently weigh larger in your heart—join me on a path I continue to travel. It will be an honor for me to walk with you for a time.

We are pilgrims and outcasts, but we pursue a city where we will find rest and be welcomed as faithful servants. Come walk with me awhile if your heart yearns to be captured by God's glory.

My children were incensed when dinnertime came and food was not on the table. My wife was gone for the weekend, and my children were, rightfully, terrified at the prospect of starvation. Of course, I knew dinner was on my shoulders, but I forgot that dinner does not waltz out of the refrigerator all prepared and warm to the serving plate for our benefit. Someone must labor behind the scenes long before the final product is presented to the expectant family.

If this workbook was to be served to you piping hot and potentially life-giving, then it needed better hands than mine to prepare it. It has passed through the hands of many fine cooks who have labored well for the sake of serving a good meal. Al and Nita Andrews read the material and offered countless important suggestions, worked on the issues related to running groups, and helped me formulate the "For Men Only" questions. Their help was invaluable. My wife, Rebecca, listened to me mutter and talk out loud as I read through each question. Her patience and perceptive remarks are interwoven throughout the finished product.

Also, scattered throughout this workbook in unshaded boxes are the personal reflections of former clients and friends. If you can imagine how it would feel to write down your shame in black and white, then mail it to a publisher to be printed—even anonymously—then perhaps you will join me in applauding their courage and their desire to do anything they can for fellow strugglers.

The NavPress staff—particularly Traci Mullins, Nancy Burke, and Bruce Nygren— were instrumental in encouraging and supporting this project. The real thanks, however, goes to the gourmet chef who conceived, wrote, and edited the project in its entirety: Karen Lee-Thorp. She engaged her excellent mind and sensitive soul in a task that required enormous personal and professional energy. Her depth of understanding of *The Wounded Heart* helped me better understand what I was trying to accomplish in the book. To whatever degree this workbook is helpful to your growth in grace, she is to be richly thanked.

Finally, I would like to thank the countless men and women I have been privileged to work with in counseling, sexual abuse recovery groups, and interactions at seminars. Your lives continue to marvel, confront, and haunt me with your courage and passion to grapple with a dark, fallen world. Even more, your passion to wrestle with God to comprehend the blessing of forgiveness compels me to weather the sea of heartache with hope that the sun of righteousness will again dawn with splendor and power.

CHAPTER ONE

GETTING STARTED

You've done what many people never find the courage to do: you've picked up a workbook on sexual abuse. Chances are that you know or suspect that this topic is relevant to you. This workbook is designed for use by women and men who know or suspect that they have been sexually abused. If you are considering this workbook for a friend or relative, you might want to read through it before you give it to your loved one. The more knowledgeable you are about what your friend is going through, the more able you will be to support him or her in the process. And perhaps you may find some of the issues touching your own heart.

If you are considering using this workbook for yourself, your decision is even more courageous. You're considering not just reading about abuse, but actually grappling with the ways abuse has affected you personally. For many people, the most difficult step toward recovery is deciding to label that suffocating shadow that looms over your past as "sexual abuse" or even "incest." Why is that step so hard? We'll explore that in chapter 2.

If you decide to use this workbook, you'll need a copy of the 1995 revised edition of the book *The Wounded Heart* by Dan Allender, if you have not done so already. The exercises in this workbook will refer to ideas explained in the book, and you'll probably want to refer to the book frequently as you move through the workbook. Either before or after completing this chapter of the workbook, you should read pages 11-46 of *The Wounded Heart, 1995 revised edition.*

What's Your Agenda?

Before you decide to use this workbook, you should know where we are coming from. If you disagree with the assumptions that underlie this workbook, then naturally you won't want to waste further time on it. If you aren't willing to make the commitments that we think will make the workbook most helpful to you, then we'd advise you to put it away for a while. (But of course we know you'll do whatever you want.)

Basic Assumptions

1. Our goal in this workbook is to help you grow more loving toward God and others, not to help you alleviate pain. We assume that your ultimate goal is love, not pain-relief.

2. Growth always involves time and struggle. Strong commitment and plenty of knowledge are valuable, but they won't make time and struggle unnecessary.

3. The time frame for growth is a lifetime. We speak of *growth,* not *recovery,* because strictly speaking, *recovery* suggests that it is possible to fully recover from the effects of evil on our lives.[1] But we sadly acknowledge that our disease is incurable and terminal. We will die of it. Yet in Francis Schaeffer's words, we can hope for "substantial healing" in this life, and total recovery in heaven.

4. The struggle we face is threefold. (a) We struggle with ourselves: Who am I? Why am I here? Why do I do the things I do? How can I change? (b) We struggle with others: given that people hurt us, how should we deal with them? (c) We struggle with God, for if God did not exist, we would be attached to nobody, responsible to nobody, limited by nobody's rules. We would be free to do whatever we like, and we would like that freedom very much.

5. Change is inevitable if our hearts are willing to struggle with self, others, and God. We have confident hope of becoming like the priceless woman: "She is clothed with strength and dignity; she can laugh at the days to come" (Proverbs 31:25).

Basic Commitments

1. I will go at the speed that is suited for me. I realize that will be slower than I would prefer. I am even willing to go through this workbook several times, each time facing the issues by asking tougher and deeper questions of myself.

2. I will not use this workbook to damage or judge myself. If I find myself doing that, I will put this workbook away until I can use it for good.

3. I will move in whatever direction seems consistent with God's plan for me. If that means putting this workbook away for a time or going very slowly, I will do that, rather than gutting it through to the end. I don't get points for finishing the workbook.

4. At some point I will open the door to community to help me in my struggle. I will allow another person to see my struggle, and I won't make myself do it all alone.

> "I have been fortunate to find a friend. . . . She and I have talked through hours and hours of experiences. She acts as my mirror; she has been impactable and accepts me as much as anyone I have known. She has the integrity to deal with our relationship and how we relate to one another. . . . I do not believe I would be this far if it were not for this relationship. It has given me the experience of being known and accepted anyway."

How Does This Workbook Work?

This workbook is designed to be used by individuals and groups who want to grow freer from the effects of sexual abuse. If you are thinking about meeting with others to discuss the exercises, watch for the gray boxes later in this chapter. Gray boxes contain help for groups.

You'll also notice unshaded boxes off to one side of the exercises. An unshaded box contains the thoughts of another victim[2] on one of the issues discussed in an exercise near it. Sometimes reading how someone else puts his or her experiences into words can help you see a way to put your own thoughts into words.

This workbook is for both men and women who want to address the issues of sexual abuse. The questions are written for both genders, but there are times when a question is better suited for a woman than a man. We encourage men to ponder the statements that are written for women. A better understanding of women is not only worthwhile for dealing with women, it will also shed light on issues that are similar for a man.

At other times we found it helpful to focus some of the questions more directly on the male experience. Those questions are labeled "For Men Only."

Some of the exercises ask you to answer a question or fill out a checklist. You can take as long as you need on those. Don't feel compelled to choose one of the items in a list as being true for you. Maybe nothing in a given list applies to you. We haven't included "Other" or "None of the above" as possible responses in every case, but if "None of the above" is true for you, write in what's true! Also, checking items in a list is not necessarily "proof" that you have been sexually abused. Persons who have not been abused could check several of the items listed under question 1 in this section, for example.

In addition, many chapters include at least one chance to do journal writing. In journal writing, you set a timer, and during that block of time you write everything that comes into your mind. You don't stop writing until the timer sounds, and you don't censor what you write. You forget about grammar, punctuation, and spelling. You don't cross out words and change them, but you can write the new thought as well. If you run out of thoughts, you can write "I'm blank. I can't think of anything to say. This is frustrating." until you have more to write.

If you are a perfectionist or critical of yourself, this kind of journal writing will be a healthy challenge for you. It will give you a chance to find out what is really going on inside your head underneath your filters of "I should think this" and "It would be more godly to feel that." Free journal writing is great for surfacing thoughts you weren't aware of. It's no news to God what you are really thinking, so you might as well know too.

Setting a time limit should make it easier to throw yourself into the writing. You can survive twenty minutes if you know you can quit then.

If you are visual, artistic, or prefer pictures to words, you can replace journal writing with some kind of picture-making, or you can do both. You can draw a picture, paint, or make a collage. You can use crayons on newsprint to write your journal exercises and vary the colors as your feelings change. We've provided space in this workbook for journaling, but you can do those exercises in a separate notebook, on canvas—wherever you like.

If you crave control, isn't it good that you have so much control over how you use this workbook? You can skip over exercises that are side issues for you and focus on the ones currently surfacing in your life. You can determine the time, place, and circumstances in which you will do exercises.

Where Am I Today?

Before you set out into unknown territory, it's worthwhile to find on a map the place you are starting from. Change is a process; and nobody goes through it in the same order, at the same speed, or in the same way as anybody else.

We bring all of our beliefs and experiences, good and bad, to the table when we read any book. Those are the lenses through which we read. You now know the assumptions and biases behind the shaping of this workbook. Now, what are your assumptions and biases? This section will help you become aware of them.

1. Put a check mark beside any of these statements that are true of you.

_____ Someone gave me this workbook, and I'm checking it out.

_____ Someone recommended this workbook to me, so I'm checking it out.

_____ I've joined or started a group for abuse victims, and we're going to use this workbook.

_____ I'm not sure if I've been sexually abused, but I know something is wrong.[3]

_____ I'm sure I've been sexually abused, but I don't know who did it.

_____ I'm sure I've been abused, but I don't have any clear memories.

_____ I'm just beginning to have memories of having been abused.

_____ I've had memories for a long time, but I'm just starting to label them "sexual abuse."

_____ I've had memories for a long time, but I'm just starting to think the abuse has damaged me.

_____ I don't think sexual abuse has affected me very much. I'm not convinced I need this workbook.

_____ I'm not sure what happened to me counts as sexual abuse.

I'm feeling . . .

_____ skeptical	_____ sad
_____ hopeful	_____ fearful
_____ hopeless	_____ confused
_____ angry	_____ desperate

_____ proud of myself for even looking at this workbook

_____ Other (name it):

_____ I don't know what I'm feeling.

_____ I've been working on the issues of abuse for quite a while. I want to know how far I've come and what's next.

_____ I've dealt with a number of abuse issues, but there are some specific areas I want to work on.

_____ I don't know how to begin to deal with sexual abuse.

_____ I don't want _____ to know I have this workbook.

_____ I don't think my past is my problem. I think I just need to believe God more.

_____ I don't think God works through workbooks.

_____ I'm hoping this workbook will take away my pain if I work hard enough.

_____ I'm approaching this workbook cynically and critically. I'm looking for the flaws.

_____ This workbook had better not make me hurt. If it does, I won't use it.

_____ I expect to be done with my struggles over abuse when I'm finished with this workbook.

2. Below, write what you have already done to pursue recovery from sexual abuse. This list should encourage you; you've probably already made some progress. Even getting this far in this workbook is more than a great many people do.

I've admitted to myself that I was abused. I've started reading this workbook.

3. Complete this sentence:

I am likely to hurt _____ with this guide by:
                       (myself/others)

I am likely to hurt myself and others when I pursue memories. I want them, but I am likely to curse my naive trust of others, distance myself from my spouse, and resort to overeating to submerge the memories. I am prone to embellish on memories with my imagination.

Where Do I Want to Go?

As you look back over your answers to questions 1 through 3, we hope you have a clearer idea of where you are now. With that information in mind, consider where you want to go.

4. What do you want to accomplish with this workbook? What do you hope will happen with the way you deal with each of the following?

YOURSELF

OTHERS

GOD

"I get the sense that my longings and desires are shameful and that a Holy God most probably is disgusted by my banal, no, repugnant thoughts and feelings."

5. As you pursue these goals, what do you expect will be your struggles with each of these?

YOURSELF

I'll have to work against being impatient and rushing myself.

OTHERS

I'll have to keep this workbook in my desk at the office so that my wife won't see it before I'm ready to talk with her about it.

*It will be hard to trust another powerful authority figure while I'm thinking
about how authority figures have betrayed me in the past.
It will be hard for me to let myself be angry with God.*

> "I've been a Christian for years, and I used to get along with God fine. Since I've started dealing with abuse, though, I've flipped out. Sometimes I'm afraid to pray with my eyes closed. When I try to pray, I usually roll up into a tight ball, hugging my knees, as though I'm bracing myself against attack. I know what the Bible says about God, but I can't get my body to believe it."

How Can I Feel Safe?

This workbook will raise painful memories and issues. You may experience feelings you've never had before or feelings you think are bad or scary. You may feel unfamiliar sensations in your body. Something that happens to you may trigger a memory, and you may react in ways that aren't typical for you. You may feel overwhelmed, sleepless, scatterbrained, or overly sensitive. If so, you're not losing your mind (at least not permanently). If you've been trying to bury memories and feelings in locked trunks in the basement of your soul, there may be chaos while the locks break and the contents of the trunks come pouring out.

We'd like to exhort you not to flee from this process, though we know you will. However, you might flee less if you take some steps to make the process survivable.

Many abuse victims don't know how to say no. We feel we can't set limits for others ("I want to keep that private for now"; "I can't do that for you") or for ourselves ("I should be able to get through at least a chapter of this workbook every week, so I'll be done by . . ."; "Why am I still struggling with this? Why can't I just give it to God and get on with life?"). But the reality is *we are limited*. We can't do everything everybody wants us to do as quickly as we and they think we should do it.

Furthermore, many of us have never felt safe. Or we've felt safe for a while until that safety was betrayed. So we invest a lot of energy into keeping ourselves safe or being anxious when we don't feel safe.

Limits and safety aren't necessarily wrong. Some limits are selfish; and many ways of protecting ourselves are unloving. But sometimes setting a limit is merely humbly facing the fact that we are not superhuman. You are entering a process that will demand time and energy. At this raw and uncertain outset, you can set some legitimate boundaries, some ground rules. As you gain courage in the upward climb, you may change some of those rules, but for now you should not feel guilty about being weak and imperfect.

If you are using this workbook on your own, set your own ground rules. If you are using it with a group, come to an agreement about rules that cover what happens in the group. You don't need to make ground rules for issues that don't bother you.

6. Look at the list of basic commitments we suggested in the box above. What basic commitments are you willing to make while you are using this guide? Will you commit yourself to any we listed? Do you want to make some other commitments?

I will not commit suicide while I am using this guide.
I will keep myself from being victimized again while using this guide by. . . .

7. Reread the guidelines for journal writing on page 13 of this workbook. Set a timer or alarm clock for twenty minutes. From now until the timer sounds, write on this page and the following page. Try to keep writing to the following page, even if you go blank for a minute. (If you're a good typist, typing can be a great way to prevent writer's cramp in your hands. But don't type if you'll have to think about the typing.)

The topic for this first journal exercise is *how you're feeling about this guide*. What are you encouraged about? Discouraged? What scares you? What are you hoping for? What are you afraid to hope for? What are you still uncertain about? What do you feel like doing after going through this chapter? What do you intend to do?

You don't have to answer all of these questions. They are intended to spark your thinking.

Continue journal writing on this page.

NOTES

1. Some Christians view John 10:10, Romans 6:13, and 2 Corinthians 5:17 as promising full recovery from the effects of evil in this life. I disagree (see pages 158-159 of *The Wounded Heart*, 1995 revised edition). Just as Paul was able to experience both abundant life and a "thorn in the flesh" that would not go away, as well as much suffering and poverty, so we, too, will continue to suffer the effects of evil while growing in joy and abundant life. It is a paradox, but a thoroughly biblical one.

2. After much thought, we have chosen to use the word *victim* rather than *survivor*. Both terms have their pros and cons. The trouble with *victim* is that it conveys the sense that we are still helpless to grow freer of the effects of our abuse, and that we are not at all responsible even for our actions as adults. Clearly, we do have the power to make choices for healing and to take responsibility for our lives. The trouble with *survivor* is that it implies that we survived our abuse intact. But most of us will admit that the state of our lives shows we may have survived physically and avoided going completely over the edge, but we are far from intact. On balance, we find *victim* to be the preferable word because it takes our damaged state more seriously and humbly, and it carries less of the independent bravado we associate with *survivor*.

3. Questions throughout this workbook assume you have some memories of sexual abuse. If you have no memories, be cautious in using this workbook. Please read "A Question of Memory" in *The Wounded Heart*, pages 21-39. This workbook uses a variety of techniques, such as journal writing, to help you clarify your memories, but if you have no memories of sexual abuse, please do not use this workbook to jump to conclusions. If your counselor has given you this workbook, be sure you understand why he or she suspects that you have been sexually abused.

4. From page 22 of this workbook, Aimee Rae Ellington, "Mixed Messages," previously unpublished poem, used by permission.

For Group Discussion

In your next group meeting, plan to devote most of the time to telling your stories. You may want to write something down to organize your thoughts, but try to tell the story without reading it to the group. If you feel you will be distant, like a news reporter in some parts, feel free to omit those parts. The group will be far more honored if you are present while you speak. It harms our souls to give the facts and nothing but the facts. It soils beauty and even resembles abuse to feel compelled by others to report your soul from a detached corner of the room.

If you can't recall details or events as you think of your story, feel free to give a verbal sketch of what your home life was like. What was it like with your parents and other relatives? Include what you wish your family had been like. How does this home life affect you on a day-to-day basis as an adult? The rationale for giving your story to the group is not that you remember everything. The agenda is simply, Will you invite the group to enter your story? Will you be present emotionally? The group will feel invited, not by the level of your articulation or the clarity of your memories, but by the offering of your heart.

Hence, don't feel pressured to tell your whole story to people you hardly know. Tell what you can. Perhaps in a few weeks your group will want to set another span of time aside to tell your stories at a deeper level. Or your stories may unfold as you discuss the workbook questions.

MIXED MESSAGES[4]
by Aimee Rae Ellington

MIXED MESSAGES
   MIXED MESSAGES
      MIXED MESSAGES

Dinner is served.
   "All is well."
      All is not well!
  "Stop whimpering! You are fine!"
    I am NOT fine.
       NO, I'M IN PAIN!!!
  "Sit down and eat your supper!"
    It hurts to sit down
      can't you tell
         didn't you hear my screams
          can't you feel my PAIN???

"Clean up your plate.
   Don't you appreciate how hard your mother worked,
     how good she is to fix such a nice meal for you?"
    I can't eat.
      I think I'm going to throw up!!!
"Shame on you,
  you naughty little girl,
    not showing appreciation
      for all your mother does for you!"
      APPRECIATION
       Mother, where are you?
         Where are you when I need you?
         Don't you hear my cries?
         I need YOU
         I want YOU
           I want love,
             not food.

Food wins out.
   Fat sets in.
Perhaps food and fat
   will numb the PAIN.
Perhaps food and fat
   will calm the FEAR.
All is not well.
   But who will hear my cries?
     Who will respond to my pain?

CHAPTER TWO

SECONDARY SYMPTOMS

Reading the Clues

Secondary symptoms are what usually draw a person to ask for help: depression, addictions, sexual dysfunction, and so on. For most of us, it is the pain of such symptoms and of failed relationships, not a zeal for holiness, that drives us to face the damage of abuse.

Usually, we've already tried to attack the symptom directly and have failed.We've failed because these symptoms are secondary—they are the ugly fruit of a diseased root. We can pick this fruit off as fast as it grows, but we'll never get better fruit until we tackle the root: our struggles with God and others.

Why look at symptoms at all, then? First, they tell us in the face of our doubt and denial that abuse occurred and that it *did* damage us. If we don't remember the actual events, or if we're tempted to tell ourselves it wasn't that bad, or if someone else assures us that we were happy as children, the symptoms stand as silent witnesses to the truth. Nobody wakes up one morning and decides to be frigid. If we have only symptoms and no memories, it's possible that something other than sexual abuse could be prompting the symptoms. There are many causes of a general symptom like depression; without memories of sexual abuse, we should be careful about jumping to conclusions. But if we have memories (even "little" ones) and symptoms, there is some statistical probability that they're connected.

Second, symptoms point to the specific areas of struggle we need to uproot. And finally, many symptoms are serious enough to warrant seeing a therapist or psychiatrist. This chapter will be a quick overview of some common symptoms associated with sexual abuse:

- Depression
- Sexual dysfunction
- Addictions and compulsions
- Eating disorders
- Physical complaints
- Low self-esteem
- Self-destructiveness

The questions are not intended to give you a diagnosis such as a therapist could give. Nor are they intended to give you proof that you have been sexually abused. Many people struggle with these symptoms for reasons other than past sexual abuse. Rather, the questions are meant to spark your awareness that something might be wrong. If you find yourself answering yes very often in one or more sections, you might consider seeing a therapist for a more rigorous diagnosis.

Before completing the questions, read pages 157-167 of *The Wounded Heart*. Some of it won't make sense until you've dealt with shame and contempt. We are raising the issue of symptoms now so you can address them with a therapist if necessary so they won't be undermining your work in the rest of this workbook. However, since the symptoms are rooted in the damage of your abuse, they probably won't go away until you've addressed that damage.

Don't worry if you can't explain the reasons behind your symptoms (such as those in questions 5 and 8). Just keep the questions in the back of your mind as you proceed through the workbook.

Depression[1]

1. Have either of these symptoms been present nearly every day for at least two weeks?

____ I feel sad, "down in the dumps."

____ I've lost interest or pleasure in all or almost all of the things I usually do (work, hobbies, etc.).

If either of these is true, continue. If not, you probably don't have a depressive illness.

2. Mark any of these that have been true nearly every day for at least two weeks.

____ I feel fatigued. I've lost my energy.

____ I've lost my appetite and/or I've lost weight.

____ My appetite is increased and/or I've gained weight.

____ I'm having trouble sleeping.

____ I'm sleeping too much.

____ I feel restless mentally or physically.

____ I'm definitely slowing down physically.

____ My interest or pleasure in sex has decreased.

____ I'm thinking slowly. I can't seem to make decisions. I can't seem to concentrate.

____ I feel the weight of the world on my shoulders.

____ It seems that no one is both willing and able to help me in my struggle with life.

____ I don't hold much hope that things will be better in the future.

____ I swing between feeling helpless/alone/unworthy and feeling cheated/abandoned/angry.

____ I think about being dead or wanting to be dead or killing myself.

If you checked at least one of the statements in question 1, *and* if you checked at least four in question 2, you may well have a depressive illness, and you should probably see a qualified professional. If you checked just two in question 2, you might consider seeing a therapist anyway. If you checked fewer than two, you can skip questions 3 and 4.

"Depression can be understood as absorbed, self-annihilating hatred toward the soul for feeling alive and then being disappointed" (*The Wounded Heart*, page 162).

3. In your childhood home, what happened when you expressed longings, disappointment, or anger? (Or, what would have happened if you had expressed those?)

"What is denied in depression is the accuracy of one's intuition that injustice has occurred, the legitimacy of one's longing for justice, and the knowledge of what would right the wrong" (*The Wounded Heart*, page 162).

4. If you think you are depressed, can you think of any disappointments in your life right now that might lie behind feelings of depression in you?

Remember, many people struggle with depression for reasons other than sexual abuse, but a high percentage of abuse victims report some level of depression.[2]

For Group Discussion

Instead of discussing every question, each person should have a chance to tell the following:

- What symptoms do you identify in yourself?
- What do you think you are getting out of each symptom? How does it give you relief from pain? What does it protect you from? How does it help you get back at someone?

When everyone has explained his or her symptoms, consider this: How does it affect you to know that you are getting something from your symptoms? What are you going to do with the knowledge of your symptoms?

Take some time to tell God what you're getting from your symptoms and how you'd like Him to work in your lives.

Sexual Dysfunction

5. Which (if any) of these sexual dysfunctions do you face?

_____ I'm hardly there at all during sex.

_____ I focus on other activities during sexual involvement.

_____ I fantasize being with other partners.

_____ Flashbacks of abuse occur during sexual involvement.

_____ I have contemptuous, abusive, or violent thoughts during sexual involvement.

_____ I'm not really interested in sex, although when I do have it, I enjoy it enough.

_____ Sex disgusts me.

_____ I don't have orgasms.

_____ It takes so much effort to achieve orgasm that it hardly seems worth it.

_____ My vagina doesn't lubricate.

_____ My vagina is so tight that intercourse is painful.

_____ I have premature ejaculation.

_____ I achieve an erection less than 70 percent of the time.

_____ I make excuses for not having sex.

"Lack of interest is often the soul's quiet rebellion to avoid the hidden memories and vague feelings that are stirred during sexual contact and arousal.

"Disgust, on the other hand, is a more pronounced and active defense. . . . Disgust might be toward one's own body for feeling aroused, toward one's partner for being too masculine or feminine, or not masculine or feminine enough, or toward men or women in general" (*The Wounded Heart*, page 163).

6. If you feel uninterested or disgusted with sex, what do you think you might be rebelling or defending against? What kind of revenge might you be achieving?

Addictions and Compulsions

"The abused man or woman often handles the confusion of the soul by drowning his or her wounds in addictive activities. *Addictive behavior is the use of any object or repetitive mode of functioning to handle stress, struggle, or sorrow that both impairs personal functioning and relationships and cannot be stopped without extensive outside intervention*" (*The Wounded Heart*, page 154).

7. Do you think you are addicted to any object or behavior (work, a person, food, masturbation, alcohol, perfectionism, etc.)? If so, list as many of your addictions as you can.

8. Are any of the following sexual addictions true of you?

_____ I like having homosexual sex.

_____ I pursue homosexual connections.

_____ I feel compelled to exhibit my genitals to others.

_____ I feel compelled to have homosexual sex.

_____ I like exhibitionism.

_____ I like voyeurism.

_____ I like sex with children.

> "In the moment of physical pleasure and having someone enjoy and accept me, I was temporarily free from the emptiness that was an undercurrent of my life. It is not surprising that sexual addictions later developed, which continued to fuel a cycle of reinforcing and intensifying my self-contempt and shame, while momentarily providing relief from them."

_____ I fight engaging in actions that set a child up for my sexual gratification.

_____ I'm a transvestite.

_____ I need to have sex every day.

It comes as startling news to many people that they are addicted to a substance or behavior not primarily because they were born sensitive to that substance. The driving force behind most addictions is that we get something from that activity that we strongly desire. If you've felt enslaved to alcohol or starving yourself, you may wonder what you could possibly be getting out of your addiction that is worth the agony you are suffering. But in fact there is almost certainly something in your heart driving your compulsion, such as a desire to . . .

- escape from pain by numbing yourself;
- feel larger than life, powerful;
- take revenge on someone;
- feel in control of your world.

9. We'll explore addictions and compulsions in depth in chapter 7. For now, give the idea some thought. Is it possible that you get something from your addiction(s) that keeps you attached to them? Explain.

Eating Disorders

10. If you identify with two or more of the following traits you are susceptible to an eating disorder and should seek counseling help. Eating disorders can quickly become life-threatening.

_____ If I don't get my full regimen of exercise, I am irritable or depressed.

_____ I exercise vigorously more than six hours per week.

_____ I panic when I overeat. I make tradeoffs for the calories—such as fasting for a period of time, vomiting, or a prescribed amount of exercise.

_____ In my life food has seemed to provide a replacement for relationships.

_____ I have food-related behaviors, such as hiding food or eating large portions rapidly that I prefer others not to know about.

_____ When I feel bloated from eating too much, I take laxatives or diuretics.

_____ I binge on food and then purge the food from my system more than three times per week.

11. Read the poem, "Mixed Messages," on page 22 of this workbook. What feelings and thoughts does it raise in you?

Physical Complaints

Many victims fight memories and effects of their damage with physical responses to their inner pain, such as back pain and headaches.

12. Do you have any chronic physical complaints that you think might be responses to the stress of blocking memories and emotional pain? If so, list them.

Of course, not all back pain or headaches are attributable to sexual abuse, so you should consider other factors as well.

Self-Esteem

13. Which (if any) of these sound like you?

_____ I undercut, devalue, and sabotage my life and deeds.

_____ I feel unworthy and guilty for every kindness to me.

_____ I often grab defeat from the jaws of victory.

_____ I feel I have to be adored by everyone or I'm upset.

Self-Destructiveness

14. Do any of these sound like you?

_____ I have a persistent thought that I will die or kill myself.

_____ I release the things I hate most about myself by cutting myself. I feel emotional less when I have plenty of physical pain.

Vital Signs

At the end of most chapters from now on, you'll find a question or two that asks you to reflect on how you are responding to what you are reading and writing. This may seem like a silly thing to do—after all, you are writing your responses, aren't you? But abuse victims are notorious for ignoring or mislabeling how we are really feeling. Reflecting on our feelings, in addition to just our thoughts, can be a helpful way of breaking through our denial.

Many of us have so deadened ourselves from pain and have fled so far from our abused bodies that we have trouble feeling anything in our bodies at all. Some of us don't notice fatigue, others overlook hunger, and still others don't think much about our physical state from one day to the next. Many victims have a difficult time letting sexual arousal build to fulfillment. Others experience arousal in confusing or harmful situations. Our bodies often seem to disturb or betray us.

Why are body-deadness and overlooking feelings so common for victims of abuse? It's all part of denying or minimizing pain, the survival strategy that kept us from completely losing our minds during the abuse. The feelings in our bodies and our emotions seemed like enemies because they tortured us, so we banished them to the dungeons of our hearts.

We'll explore this kind of denial further in later chapters. Until then, we'll try periodically to notice what is happening in our bodies and emotions. Does your body feel hot or cold? Are you shaking? Are your muscles relaxed or tense? How is your stomach? Your head? Are you aware of sexual feelings and arousal? We will try to help you better understand the physical effects of your inner world.

If you have trouble feeling anything or labeling what you feel, we hope you'll heap as little contempt upon yourself for failing as you can possibly manage. (We know it is unreasonable to expect you not to beat on yourself at least a little bit, since that reaction comes automatically to you.) One helpful clue to how you're feeling is what you feel like doing. What would you normally do in this situation? Eat a pint of ice cream? Wage war on the forces of dirt and untidiness in your kitchen? Bury yourself in a romance novel or TV show? Go running or weightlifting? Start another project at work or at home?

15. How are you feeling right now after reflecting on these symptoms in your life? What sensations, if any, are you aware of in your body?

16. What do you feel like doing?

17. What would you like to say to God right now?

NOTE

1. This inventory is adapted from material in *The Wounded Heart*; and Donald F. Klein, M.D., and Paul H. Wender, M.D., *Do You Have a Depressive Illness?* (New York: Plume Books, 1988), pages 7-8.

2. Refer to pages 282-288 of *The Wounded Heart*, notes section of chapter 8.

CHAPTER THREE

FACING THE BATTLE

Denial

A problem cannot be solved until it has first been faced. A major shift occurs when words are given to what is known or suspected to be true: *I have been sexually abused.* The enormous battle in labeling the truth is difficult to imagine. We are deeply reluctant to begin the process of change by admitting that damage has occurred.

Refusing to face what is true is called *denial*. Denial means we don't like the way God behaves or the reality He has made, so we construct a god and a reality more to our taste. We have many convincing reasons to avoid having memories and labeling them as abuse: facing the truth will plunge us into the anguish of grief, anger, and shame; it will shatter our illusions about our childhood; it will demand changes in the ways we live now; it will cast floodlights on some of our current relationships; it will throw our lives into an uproar.

If you've gotten this far, you are at least entertaining the possibility that you have been damaged by abuse. If you have been dealing with these issues for some time, you may be aware that words like *shredded* and *poisoned* seem more appropriate for what you've suffered than *damaged.* If you've just begun, you may be aware of only the tip of an iceberg.

> "At first I thought I was reluctant to admit the abuse because it seemed silly—ridiculous—to let a couple of ten- to fifteen-minute incidents be such a big deal. My parents, especially my dad, always told me that I was too sensitive anyhow. . . . As I later discovered, I didn't admit to a good portion of earlier abuse because so much of it was 'underground' that I didn't recognize it as such for a long time. The other reason was that my parents, in fact, had covertly set me up for the overt abuse. How could I *dare* implicate my parents?"

Before you go on, read pages 46-56 and 189-213 in the book *The Wounded Heart.* Some of the later material may not be entirely clear until you've read the rest of the book, but it will give you a taste of what to expect in this workbook and offer some general guidelines for pursuing change. It will also explain concepts like denial and the use and misuse of memories, both of which you'll want to understand as you work through this chapter. Also, read "A Question of Memory" on pages 21-39 of the book.

Page 48 of *The Wounded Heart* defines sexual abuse like this:

Sexual abuse is any contact or interaction (visual, verbal, or psychological) between a child/adolescent and an adult when the child/adolescent is being used for the sexual stimulation of the perpetrator or any other person. Sexual abuse may be committed by a person under the age of eighteen when that person is either significantly older than the victim or when the perpetrator is in a position of power or control over the victimized child/adolescent.

Page 51 of the book lists types of sexual abuse. At this point, however, you may be battling whether or not abuse occurred, or if it was really that damaging. It is comforting to know that change does not depend on "resolving" or "healing" the past—it depends on facing what is true. If your heart is open, over time God will bring what He desires for you to see to your awareness.

Ironically, our greatest hope lies in facing how bad things really are. Life really is lousy a lot of the time. People really have never loved us the way we long to be loved. Abuse, at various levels of intensity, is a daily occurrence. As the Bible says, "Dear friends, do not be surprised at the painful trial you are suffering, as though something strange were happening to you" (1 Peter 4:12). Oddly enough, when we finally become willing to admit the worst, we can laugh in the teeth of evil because we know that in the end, evil does not win.

Memories

The road away from denial leads through the swamp of memories. Of the three areas we deny, the first is our past. It feels as though memories are our enemy because they prove that the pretty, happy world we'd like to believe we grew up in was neither pretty nor happy. We don't like to think of ourselves as victims who were not well loved. We prefer to minimize: "It wasn't that bad. Other people have had a much worse childhood."

Questions arise: Is there something inherently healing in remembering and talking about the past abuse? How much do we need to remember in order to heal? What does it mean to tell our stories? Is it wise to pursue memories?

> "I had no memories of sexual abuse and no reason to believe I had been abused until about four years ago, when in my early fifties my husband and I went to N. for marital counseling. The night before we were to meet with him, I had a pre-sleep impression of being in my bedroom as a child and a figure came and bent over my bed. I was terrified. It seemed like it was my dad. During that first counseling session I wondered out loud, 'What if . . . ?' I ended up sobbing."

When we begin to face our abuse, most of us have only fragments of memories, a few pieces of a jigsaw puzzle. The truth is, more often than not, even when we are well down the road of growth, we still have large gaps in our puzzle.

Why don't memories come back more easily? Perhaps because God has our welfare in mind (although His behavior infuriates us and may make us doubt this fact strongly). Perhaps God allows only as much memory as we are ready for. He will not allow a memory to come if He knows we will use it to punish ourselves or others.

Memories should not be either rejected or pursued as villains. Rather, each piece of the puzzle should be honored as a guest. "Thank you for coming. What can you teach me? How can I grow from knowing you? I want to spend some time with you alone." If each guest is honored, each morsel thoroughly chewed and digested, God may be more willing to send us more guests and morsels. But if we spit on the memories He sends and at the same time demand ten times as many, we can hardly be surprised if our memories are blocked.

Also, memories are more likely to come when we are obeying God and moving toward others, as opposed to when we are huddled in our caves racking our brains for memories and keeping the world away.

We must also be open to the possibility that there are no incidents of sexual abuse to remember other than what we already remember. It's possible that an eerie feeling about someone is not based on having been molested by that person. The key with memories is to avoid a fierce demand: "*I must* remember something!" The exercises in this workbook offer opportunities to retrieve what is actually stored in your brain; please don't use them to imagine what is not there.

Some authorities recommend that memories not be pursued because of the danger that recovered memories may be false. I believe there is no reason to fear a *responsible* process of memory pursuit. Responsible pursuit includes a willingness to remember little or nothing as well as a willingness to remember a lot. And it includes a commitment to seek other evidence that confirms or disconfirms our memories.

You should know that the younger you were when you were abused, the less likely you are to recover full memories. Children under the age of three generally have insufficient brain development to store what is called "episodic" memory—that is, memory of events. They are, however, strongly affected by those events.

1. We can begin by honoring the guests we already have. What fragmentary memories of abuse do you already have? What reasons do you have to believe you were or might have been sexually abused? Even if you have no clear memories, something motivated you to pick up this guide. An alarm buzzer went off somewhere in your gut. Write down everything you can remember and every pattern or problem in your later life that you think points toward sexual abuse.

Keep in mind that not all memories are visual. There may be a *scent* that upsets you; the *sound* of a door opening sticks in your mind; you can't bear to be *touched* in a certain way. Maybe you react to certain people in a way that seems unusual: you tend to avoid your uncle at family reunions. Think about the way your body reacts during sex, a massage, or friendly hugs.

If you don't remember much and are going on mere suspicion, that's okay at this point. Memories often come back gradually as you work through issues related to abuse. This exercise is an opportunity to write down all of your reasons for suspicion; you shouldn't let yourself be pressured to draw conclusions if your memories are fragmentary. (Chapter 11, "Honesty," of the book has more to say about memories.)

Take a few moments to tell God how you're feeling and to ask Him to bring up anything it would be helpful for you to remember at this point. Then take twenty minutes to scribble all the bits and pieces of memories you can think of. Write your thoughts on the remainder of this page and the following one; or you can use your own journal notebook. Setting a timer will give you permission to say, "That's enough for now" and stop, even if you don't feel you have remembered "enough." Before you begin, reread the guidelines for journal writing on page 13.

> "I had always had some memories, but I never thought much about them.
>
> "I worked in a battered women's shelter while in college. We had lots of literature on all kinds of abuse. I remember filing an article on incest. I looked at the word and said to myself, 'That's the word for what happened to me.' But it didn't occur to me to *read* the article, or that I might be deeply damaged by those long-ago events."

Continue journal writing on this page.

"If I hadn't written down the memories as they came, I might think I had imagined the whole thing. They seem so shadowy now, like dreams. But there are the records with dates in my journal. And of course, the mess of my whole life points to abuse."

2. Now take as long as you need to write down any reasons you have for doubting that anything happened to you, or doubting that what happened was abuse. Listen closely for the nagging whispers inside you that tell you it's all in your imagination or it was minor. Write them all down.

> "I made the typical excuses: It wasn't as bad as what some girls and women go through; it wasn't so bad that you would read about it in the newspaper. Plus, this was someone I knew, so it wasn't like something really awful had happened. . . . I didn't get raped, just molested, so I wasn't going to get pregnant."

3. If you aren't sure whether you were abused or whether a particular person was responsible, what steps can you take to confirm or disconfirm your suspicions? Are there family members, friends, or other adults you can ask? Do you have strong physical reactions to sexual stimuli that indicate disgust, an unwillingness to feel "all there," or an involuntary constriction and tightness?[1]

4. Other ways of denial include minimizing the damage and making excuses for the abuser. How (if at all) have you done either of those? Complete the sentences below.

It wasn't as bad as it might have been because . . .

> *He was gentle. . . . He wasn't really related to me. . . . I had my clothes on. . . . She never touched me.*

It wasn't as bad as it might have been because . . .

It wasn't as bad as it might have been because . . .

It wasn't as bad as it might have been because . . .

It wasn't as bad as it might have been because . . .

I can't blame my abuser because . . .

> *He was abused as a child. . . . He was under a lot of pressure. . . . He was only a teenager. . . . She needed a man around, and Dad had treated her so badly.*

"My abuser was a cousin one year older than myself. Before I came to view the experiences as abuse there was no need to make excuses for him since I viewed myself as a willing participant. What I have found in talking with many men who have had same-sex experiences in child-hood is that although one child may initiate or set the other up (the abuser), the abused one often experi-ences enjoyment and may become the initiator in future sexual experiences. When this chain of events occurs it is very difficult to view oneself as being abused."

I can't blame my abuser because . . .

I can't blame my abuser because . . .

I can't blame my abuser because . . .

I can't blame my abuser because . . .

Style of Relating

To deny or minimize our memories is to reject the truth about our past and ourselves. Our second area of denial has to do with the present: We don't want to face what other people are doing to us now and what we do to them.

Our way of interacting with others can be called our *style of relating*. "A style of relating is *the characteristic manner of both offering and protecting oneself in social interactions*" (*The Wounded Heart*, page 168). We've been hurt, and we've developed our own set of strategies for avoiding being hurt again. We doubt that we can trust God to protect us (He's done a pathetic job of doing that in the past, we feel), so we have to protect ourselves.

Chapter 10 will give you a chance to examine your style of relating in depth. For now, just try to begin noticing the main features of the way you relate.

5. Our style of relating shows most clearly when we are under stress or suffering a loss. Think of a few times when you've been stressed recently. Try to remember a time when you've suffered loss. It may take a few minutes to recall such memories.

Do you see any patterns in the way you responded in those situations? How do you typically interact with other people when you are in situations like those?

6. What is one hard thing to face about how someone close to you is treating you?

God

The past and the present—ourselves and others—are hard to deal with. But perhaps our most stubborn denial has to do with God, primarily regarding our future. What does it mean to deal with a God who has failed to protect us in the past or the present, and who promises no insurance against more suffering in this life? About our memories we wonder: Where was He? About our current relationships we ask: Where is He now? What's He doing now to help? How, then, can we trust Him for our future?

7. Make a list of every reason you can think of for you to mistrust God. Include bad ones as well as good ones. Don't tell yourself that it's ungodly to mistrust God or that there can't be any reason to mistrust Him; remember, He already knows what's in your heart. Write down everything the devil or your damaged soul could whisper to you in a vulnerable moment.

8. Now list any reasons you can think of to trust God with your future enough to lead you through the painful process of change. Write them down even if you don't find them convincing this moment.

Name the Enemy

Denial says that our memories, other people, or God is the enemy we have to combat. It would be easy to feel that the pain we've suffered or the wicked abuser is the enemy. The pain is real and important, and the abuser is a criminal, but neither is our true enemy. We can't change our abuser, and focusing on him or her only consumes a lot of energy to no avail. In fact, obsessing about our abuser begins to make us subtly more and more like him or her. Deadening the pain merely deadens our souls, while the pain lives on as the monster lurking in the basement. The terror of it is as devastating as the pain itself. (See *The Wounded Heart,* pages 57-60.)

Ultimately, the enemy is the prowling beast that attempts to devour and destroy the beauty of God's Kingdom. The enemy is denial: our inner commitment to construct reality and God according to our own desires. Whenever we immerse ourselves in dreams of having the perfect man or woman; being more beautiful, powerful, or rich than we are; or seeing others pay immediately for their crimes—whenever we feed on such fantasies, we are quietly telling God we disapprove of His reality.

9. Can you identify with the feeling, *the enemy is the pain and whatever is responsible for it*? If you can, how have you gone about fighting this enemy?

10. Have you ever acted as though your enemy were your abuser(s)? Explain.

11. Look back over your answers in this chapter. If you were to start treating denial as your archenemy, how would your way of handling life and abuse be different? What would you have to change?

Vital Signs

If it's hard for you to verbalize feelings, express yourself through pictures. Make a collage. Collect magazines, and start cutting out images and words that touch on what you're feeling. Arrange and glue them on cardboard or construction paper. When you're done, see if you can verbalize what you've tried to portray. Or, show your collage to a friend, and ask that person to tell you what he or she sees. If you like, write or talk about the feelings and thoughts that arise as you look at "Night of Fury" on the opposite page.

Some other examples of black-and-white photos of collages appear on pages 65, 87, and 138 of this workbook.

41

****

For Men Only

Many men find it difficult to make collages or use other arts-and-crafts ways of portraying their feelings. But we do think is important to gain a visual picture of your inner experience. What means do you use to express inner feelings? Some men use photography, scribble on a note pad, build furniture, or make model airplanes. Whatever means you currently use to "feel" in a visual manner, we encourage you to tailor that so you can experience and express your feelings as you go through this workbook.

****

12. When you think about not fighting or fleeing from your abuser or your pain, how do you feel? What do you feel emotionally, or in your body?

13.What do you feel like doing?

14. What would you like to say to God at this point?

Memories Again

New memories may come to you as you move through the issues in this workbook. As ugly and dirty as they may be, they come bearing valuable information. If you are not taking extreme measures to force memories, those that surface deserve to be treated with respect. As they arrive, take time to write down what you remember, the feelings each memory stirs in you, and what you learn about your damage from each of them. You may want to record all this in a separate journal.

NOTE
1. No symptom can ever be viewed as proof. Too many other experiences can be related to a given symptom. But strong physical responses to sexual stimuli point to some kind of trauma of a sexual nature.

For Group Discussion

It's not easy to stop fighting our pain and start fighting our denial. The pain is genuine and intense. What can you do to support each other in making this shift? How can you help each other face the truth and bear the pain? What would you like the other group members to do for you?

Talk about body feelings. Some group members may have made more progress than others in feeling physical and emotional messages. In fact, some may be struggling with painful physical symptoms chronically as their bodies express what their hearts can't handle. Try to identify what you're feeling right now. If that's hard, explore some reasons why you're not letting yourself feel. Why do you suppose your heart is so firmly opposed to having feelings? What are the benefits of being numb?

Consider doing collages of feelings together. Talk about what you see in one another's creations.

CHAPTER FOUR

STAGES OF ABUSE

"How is one to enter the chambers of the wounded heart that struggles below the guise of competence and congeniality? Like a labrinyth, the twisted pathway will not reveal its secrets to one who does not understand the complexity or pitfalls of the process. The wounded heart must be gently and accurately understood if it is to reveal the heartache it has stored for years. A grasp of the internal pain begins with an idea of how abuse occurs and what abuse does to the perspective of the victim" (*The Wounded Heart*, pages 91-92).

The following five sections will invite you to compare your experience of abuse with the stages outlined in the book. The fewer memories you have, the more blanks you will find yourself leaving. But that in itself can be revealing. Why would you block out memories of the setup while remembering the "abuse proper," or vice versa?

I know you may find it hard to resist feeling inadequate when you can't answer some or even most of the questions. But if you knew all the answers, you wouldn't need this workbook, right? Even *I* can't answer all of these questions adequately.

You probably already know that dredging up or focusing on these memories is often painful. The temptation to run away into a pain relieving activity (work, fantasy, eating, smoking . . .) can be enormous. It might help to give yourself time, rather than trying to complete the whole chapter in one sitting. After you complete a section, call a friend to get some support.

At times when you feel the urge to relieve your pain, it would be good to begin making a habit of turning to involvement with other people, rather than isolating yourself with your pain. Better still, ask someone to *pray* with you. Try to do something that *isn't* one of your usual pain-relief strategies, instead something that connects you with others and God.

In this chapter we will look at the different stages of abuse:

The Setting
Stage 1: Intimacy and Secrecy
Stage 2: Physical Contact that Appears Appropriate
Stage 3: Sexual Abuse Proper
Stage 4: Threats and Privileges

The Setting

Abuse doesn't occur in a vacuum. Most of us became vulnerable to abuse because of the ways our families lived. We may have concocted fantasies of a perfect childhood, but it will be hard for us to uncover the grief, rage, and terror that rule us as adults until we face the roots of that pain in our childhood homes.

1. Read pages 91-96 of the book *The Wounded Heart*. Then, in the checklist below, mark sentences that remind you of your experience as a child. If you remember little about your childhood or remember it as being quite different from what the book describes, that's okay.

> "I recently began talking with my father about how I felt as a child. He responded, 'It seems as though you feel you weren't loved. I assure you that your mother and I have always had the highest appreciation for your performance as a daughter.' Do you say thank you to a statement like that?"

_____ Our home appeared normal and good to outsiders.

_____ Relationships in our home were distant and empty (although they may have appeared proper).

_____ I had little or no healthy intimacy with family members.

_____ I was not enjoyed for who I was.

_____ I was enjoyed, if at all, only for what I did.

_____ I played the role of an adult in my family in these ways . . .

_____ I felt weighed down by adult burdens.

_____ My physical boundaries were invaded in these ways . . .

_____ My boundaries of thoughts and feelings were invaded like this . . .

_____ I found it hard to trust my perceptions and feelings.

_____ Our home was demanding, conservative, and rule-bound.

_____ Our family highly valued loyalty.

_____ I felt alone.

_____ I was committed to pleasing others.

_____ I was intertwined in the push and pull of my parents' every offer or refusal to provide love and support.

_____ I felt as if I were walking on eggs or through a minefield.

_____ I numbed myself to pain by . . .

"The dictates that what you do is the sum total of who you are, that feelings are ridiculous and that sex doesn't even exist, were incorporated into the very fiber of my being as I grew. To question, let alone explore any idea to the contrary was to beg for punishment."

_____ I was hypervigilant to prevent danger or family upset.

_____ I had an inner person and an outer person.

_____ I felt . . .

2. In what significant ways did your childhood differ from what the book describes?

3. Is there anything else that comes to mind about your childhood?

"By the time I was ten years old I felt that I was not good enough to be wanted or enjoyed for just being myself. My life was a quest to find a way to make an impact on my family that would get me the kind of love and involvement I longed for."

4. How did thinking and writing about your childhood make you feel? What do you feel like doing now?

5. If you are more visual than verbal, you might try creating a picture of your family when you were a child. You could draw or paint scenes or portraits. You could do something abstract, assigning colors to each person depending on how you felt about each. You could make a collage out of words and images cut from magazines. You could depict each person separately or in one typical scene, such as a breakfast table.

Looking at photographs may also help you. Dig through old family pictures and think about the feelings they raise in you. What feelings about childhood do they evoke in you? Write your thoughts under questions 1 through 4 or on a separate piece of paper.

Stage 1: Intimacy and Secrecy

"The first stage of abuse can be considered a conscious, intentional setup that opens the refrigerator doors to the sight and taste of a hungry child" (*The Wounded Heart*, page 97).

For Group Discussion

1. Start with how it felt to complete the checklist. Was anything confusing, frustrating, or painful? Did any group members find it hard to know what to say because you've forgotten your childhood or replaced it with fantasies?

2. Instead of merely telling what you checked, give your group a verbal portrait of what your family was like. If you're a visual person, share a picture.

3. If you have any photographs of yourself as a child or of your family or home, bring some of them to the group. Discuss how looking at them makes you and the others feel.

4. Family sculpture is a powerful technique for expressing perceptions about one's family. Assign each group member the role of one of your family members. Put each person in a physical position that depicts how they relate to each other. Two people might be facing each other nose to nose in hostility. Another might be holding out both hands in a gesture that keeps the others at a distance. Put yourself in the sculpture. Are you backing away? Holding other members upright or together? When you're done, let the rest of the group tell how they respond to your sculpture. Tell how it felt for you to make the sculpture.

   The purpose of this exercise is not to bring up new memories, nor to vent emotions. It's not "the more you lose control of yourself, the better." Rather, the goal is simply to face memories and truth that you normally wouldn't face. Your rage, for instance, isn't "good," but it is good to honestly face the fact that you are filled with unloving rage.

---

6. Read pages 97-99 of *The Wounded Heart*. Do you think your abuser set you up consciously? If so, how did he or she do it? If you don't believe so, explain why not.

7. If you did receive an offer of relationship, intimacy, special privileges, or rewards, how did you feel about the situation at that time?

8. How do you feel now when you recall those memories? What happens in your mind? In your body?

Stage 2: Physical Contact that Appears Appropriate

"The essence of Stage 2 is the beginning of physical and sensual bonding" (*The Wounded Heart*, page 99).

9. Read pages 99-102 from the book *The Wounded Heart*. Do you remember your abuser using apparently appropriate touch to heighten the bond between you or to persuade you to drop your defenses? If so, how did he or she do that?

> "No one had ever pursued me or taken a personal interest in me before, so when she took me into her home, I thought I'd died and gone to heaven. She was very affectionate and 'huggy' with me. . . . It wasn't unusual for her to climb into bed at bedtime with one of her teenaged daughters to talk and hug. . . . One night late she came into my room to talk. Then we both fell asleep. I woke up in the night with her hands all over me."

). How did you feel when it happened?

11. How do you feel now when you think about yourself trusting someone to start touching you like this? (You can answer this even if you have no precise memories of the experience.)

12. If you feel guilty for enjoying your abuser's touch, why do you suppose that is? (Do you feel shame for a sin or for some God-made part of you?)

> "I can hardly believe it when I think that even the disgusting ways this man touched me seemed an improvement over the sterile wasteland of my home."

Stage 3: Sexual Abuse Proper

"Sexual abuse is the final blow that sabotages the soul in a climactic betrayal, mocking the enjoyment of relationship and pouring contempt on the thrill of passion.

"The betrayal involves more than relational sabotage. It is also intensely personal and physical. . . . The tragedy of abuse is that the enjoyment of one's body becomes the basis of a hatred of one's soul" (*The Wounded Heart*, pages 103-104).

13. Read pages 102-106 of *The Wounded Heart*. Then describe what you remember of how you felt during the abuse. (Do you recall feeling anything in your body, or were you isolated from your body? Do you remember your emotions? What did you do afterward?)

14. Do you identify with the feeling of being betrayed by your body, or of simultaneously hating and wanting the person or the sensations? Explain.

> "I *let* it happen, I didn't stop her and I enjoyed the orgasm. In fact, for fifteen years I would wake up from time to time in the night with an orgasm and every time the shame would flood over me, yet I would never allow myself to think about the incident. Something was wrong with *me.*"

15. If you don't remember feeling sexually aroused, which of the following do you think is the reason why not?

____ My fear blocked arousal.

____ Physical pain overwhelmed arousal.

____ I split my mind off from my body, so I wouldn't feel anything.

____ Rage overwhelmed arousal.

____ Other (name it):

16. Do you recall feeling strong emotions (anger, terror, etc.)? Which, if any, of the following sound like you?

____ I wasn't feeling strongly about anything.

____ I was too afraid to feel anger.

____ I felt only the pleasure.

_____ I split my mind off from my body, so I wouldn't feel anything.

_____ The rage and pleasure together was too much for me, so I've blocked both.

_____ I felt angry and frightened, but no pleasure.

_____ I felt extremely angry.

17. How do you feel right now after thinking about these memories?

Stage 4: Threats and Privileges

"The final stage of abuse is in many ways similar to the first stage: the development of intimacy and secrecy. Unlike the first stage, however, the glory days are gone forever. The abuser will use whatever leverage he or she can to instill loyalty and fear in the heart of the victim to ensure silence and compliance" (*The Wounded Heart*, page 107).

18. Read pages 107-110 of *The Wounded Heart*. Do you recall your abuser giving you any threats or privileges? Describe what happened.

> "To be found out would mean total loss of respect by my father and the burden of having added pain to my already burdened mother."

19. How do you feel about yourself for letting yourself be silenced by these actions?

20. Do you think you created a new identity or history when you grew up and escaped the abusive relationship and your family? Describe what you have done to bury the past.

The Big Picture

21. How are you feeling right now about God and His role in your life, past and present? What would you like to say to God?

22. Try to pull together what you've been reflecting on. Did anything become clearer as you pieced through your memories? Where are your major gaps?

23. How does your experience of abuse differ from the classic four-stage pattern:

       Stage 1: Intimacy and Secrecy
       Stage 2: Physical Contact that Appears Appropriate
       Stage 3: Sexual Abuse Proper
       Stage 4: Threats and Privileges

24. Has it been helpful to walk through your experience in these stages? If so, how? If not, why do you suppose that's so?

CHAPTER FIVE

SHAME

Exposed

When people are victimized, denial (ignoring or rewriting the past, present, and future) is a reflex response. We immediately begin looking for ways to survive that don't include facing the ugly truth and depending utterly on God. Beneath most of our survival strategies lies an intricate and terrifying cycle of shame and contempt.

Shame is the horrible feeling that we are seen as deficient and undesirable by someone who we hope will deeply enjoy us. It starts when someone whose opinion matters to us finds out one of our dark secrets, and we are exposed.

On pages 60-75 of *The Wounded Heart*, you'll find the elements of shame outlined. *Exposure* is a key element. Shame is an experience of the eyes. There is no shame when we do something dreadful and there is no possibility of someone important finding out. But if that possibility does exist, the terror of possible future exposure is often ten times more agonizing than the shame of actually being exposed.

As fallen humans, our natural response to the fear of exposure is hiding—denial and deception. Like Adam and Eve, we cover ourselves with fig leaves and hide behind bushes against the searching eyes of God or other people. We despise standing vulnerable before God and others; therefore, we find countless ways to flee from His and their presence to avoid being seen. Most of those ways involve contempt, which we'll address in the next chapter.

> "One illustration of shame I have used about myself is that I'm in a group of people and something is written on my back. Everyone knows about it, but not one person will tell me what it says, yet they shun me for it."

Shame is a common experience for all humans. Therefore, the fact that you experience shame and can answer "yes" to many of the questions in this chapter neither proves nor disproves that you have been sexually abused. However, even if you ultimately determine that your shame has other roots, you may find this chapter helpful.

1. Most of us can recall a few embarrassing moments of childhood or adulthood that make funny stories at parties. For some of us, those shameful experiences continue to hurt so much that they have never become funny. (A few of us are so skilled at denial that we have conveniently forgotten every embarrassing moment of our whole lives.)

Embarrassment is a mild form of shame. Write down the story of one embarrassing moment you recall.

2. How do you feel when you think about that incident? What does thinking about it make you want to do?

> "I have felt ashamed of many things that remind me of being a woman. The 'filthy rags' of Isaiah 64:6 refer to cloths stained with menstrual flow, and I would have to say that 'filthy' is about the best one-word summary I can think of to describe how I feel. I have felt ashamed of wanting to be in a relationship with a man, even if the relationship is a nonsexual one. On more than one occasion I have been seen as a threat to a marriage and gotten the message that I'm dangerous. Spiritual issues aside, the thought that I could be that seductive to *any* man, let alone a married one, is absurd to me. But the idea that I'm toxic to relationships reinforces the image that perhaps I *should* be thrown away like a dirty diaper."

For many of us, our bodies began to do things at puberty that we considered shameful. Our first menstruation, erection, or nocturnal emission seemed to expose things about ourselves we wanted to keep hidden. Whether those things actually were exposed to others, or whether we only dreaded being exposed, we began to feel desperately self-conscious about our bodies.

All of our peers were changing, too, and many of us felt shame because our bodies were changing faster, slower, or in less desirable ways than others' were. We were the first or last to wear a bra, the first or last to grow pubic hair, the tallest or shortest in the class. We gained weight or had pimples. We lost control of our voice while it was changing, and embarrassed ourselves by squeaking when we tried to talk or laugh.

Some people find these topics so shameful that they would rather we didn't even put them in print. If we never think or talk about them, perhaps we can deny them out of existence.

3. What do you recall finding shameful about your body as a teenager? What did you wish no one would ever or had ever noticed about you?

> "I was ashamed of my body. To get me to have good posture, my dad would say 'stick your dukes out.' My brothers joined in."

4. What do you find shameful about your body now? What would you prefer to hide?

> "I have struggled with masturbation, and that brought shame."

5. Now make a list of the aspects of your abuse you want to keep hidden. What *don't* you want other people (or certain ones) to learn about you?

It may be scary to put your secrets into printed words. *You* don't even want to know them, and what if someone reads your workbook? Here's a chance to take a risk with God. Can He help you face your secrets? Can He protect your appropriate privacy? Ask Him.

If there are genuinely dangerous people in your world who truly might read your workbook, you can answer this question and the next few on separate paper and tear it up when you've finished the chapter.

I liked it when he touched me.
I protected him from my parents.

6. Think about each of your secrets. Why would it be terrible if people learned that secret? Write down what you are afraid of for each secret.

People would think I wanted the abuse.
My parents would be furious at me for not trusting them.

> "I was ashamed that I had an orgasm with my brother. I didn't know it was an orgasm, but I knew there was pleasure and that what I was doing was wrong."

7. a. Have you ever experienced someone treating you in a hurtful way when they learned of your abuse? If you have, what was it like? (Did they disdain or ignore you? Make light of your pain? Blame you? Try to rescue you and make the pain go away, so that you would feel grateful?)

b. How did you respond?

What Is Exposed?

Shame is best described by its parallel to a physical trauma: an internal hemorrhage. When a blood vessel erupts, we can feel the flow; something inside us has burst and we know immediately that we are losing vitality. Yet even in the emergency, we can't get to the source of the internal bleeding. All of the symptoms point to immediate death; but we are powerless to stop the hemorrhage.

Some shame is legitimate. Legitimate shame exposes our rebellion against God. We should feel shame when we have demeaned or slighted another human being, thus violating our relationships with her and the Lord. We should be heartbroken, humbled, shamed when we do not worship the Lord with our whole heart, soul, mind, and strength. Being exposed as wanting to take immediate revenge on someone or wanting to use them to fulfill our desires should stop us cold, shut our mouths, and lead to a desperate desire to change that bears no aroma of self-contempt.

But seeing that we've hurt God or others does not usually have this effect. If we're afraid of being rejected by God or others for displeasing them, we may feel shame that we've been stupid enough to get ourselves into trouble, but that is not the same as genuine brokenness.

More often, we feel shame, not about our sin, but about our humanness. We trip over our feet, lose a competition, or forget someone's name, and we feel exposed as less than perfect. Why do we feel more shame over failure than over rebellion? The first reason has to do with the god we serve. Our god has the power to determine our value and worth.

If falling short of God's standard of love shames us and drives us humbly to seek mercy, then our God truly is the Lord of grace. But if looking foolish in the eyes of other people deeply shames us, then we have given people the power to determine our worth. Likewise, if the shame of sin merely drives us to work harder to please a harsh, demanding god (or to measure up to our own prideful standards), then we are not worshiping the God of the Bible.

"I wanted to believe I was ashamed of the way I treat men because it's ungodly—it's sinful. But I finally saw that I didn't care so much about wounding God as I did about maintaining my self-image as a good Christian. A good Christian, by my standards, might have little sins. But this was a big sin, and my pride couldn't handle it."

Our identities are very loosely stitched together. Shame exposes the fragments and sinful remnants of our souls. The polished and intact image we convey to others is an effort to deny our need of God. He is the only One who can integrate the fragments of our identity. And He does this through the restoration of forgiveness, made possible by Christ's death on the cross. When we are shamed because we have failed to love, we can choose to chastise ourselves, polish our performance, and cover our tracks. Or, we can choose to respect the exposure as a gift that can guide us to productive repentance and deep gratitude for Christ.

The fact is, as bad as it is to be exposed as wounded or imperfect, it is nothing like the terror of being exposed before God as rebellious. We avoid the hideous experience of Adam and Eve at all costs. To stand in the blinding light of God's presence, naked and seared by His penetrating eyes—we fear that like nothing else. We far prefer to stage a diversion to get everyone's eyes off our rebelliousness. Often, the best diversion is a theatrical shame session about our hurts or imperfections. Oddly enough, we usually prefer to punish and shame ourselves for doing something wrong, rather than stand unexcused before God and be forced to rely on His forgiveness.

Legitimate shame is facing our failure to trust God—not just to keep our world intact, but also to keep our soul intact. The reason we fear being exposed to people is that we fear they will permanently abandon us, and we think such disgrace and abandonment will kill our soul. Illegitimate shame is a result of entrusting our soul to the wrong people—that is, anyone except God.

8. Look back at the embarrassing moments and shameful truths you've been writing about. Which of them involves letting *people* determine your value and desirability? Which of them involves letting *God* determine those things?

Put a P next to the ones that show giving empowering trust to people, and a G next to ones that show trust in God.

9. a. Can you think of a time when you welcomed the exposure of your sin? Describe it briefly.

b. What result did this event have in your life?

10. How do you tend to respond when you display your humanness in minor ways, like tripping or making a mistake?

As you progress through this workbook, pray that you will find new courage to:

- Welcome the piercing light of truth.
- Be willing to be stunned by it.
- Enjoy the refreshment of turning away from false gods.
- Rest in Christ's complete work of covering sin through the Cross.

Longing for Love

When we feel exposed as undesirable before someone who has power to judge our soul, we usually hate the part of our God-made self that has caused us pain. The part we hate most is *our longing to be wanted and enjoyed*. If we didn't want that, we think, we would not be shamed by others' rejection and abuse. We fail to see the gap between longing to be wanted by someone (which is legitimate) and staking our lives on being wanted by that person (which is idolatry). Instead of giving up the idolatry, we try to kill the longing.

9. Which of these sound like you?

_____ I don't long to be wanted and enjoyed by people, and I never have.

> "*Enjoyed* sounds so sexual, lustful, abusive. It feels like I'm being eaten with gusto."

_____ I don't feel I long to be wanted and enjoyed, but I think that deep down I do long for that.

_____ I used to long for that a lot, but now I rarely think about it.

_____ I am more aware of that longing than I used to be.

_____ I long for that intensely, but I long more to love God and others well.

_____ Being wanted and enjoyed by people is one of my top priorities, ahead of loving God and others.

10. What would you say you long for most? Complete the sentences.

I'd give anything to have . . .

I feel as though I'd really be happy if I could have . . .

The things I miss most in life are . . .

The things I don't ever want to have to live without are . . .

11. What signs do you see in your life that you have tried (and maybe succeeded) to deaden your longing for deep, satisfying involvement with others?

> *My heart clutches and backs away anytime someone gives me a really warm compliment.*

"I have had lots of very erotic dreams. Dreams and daydreams of being raped created constant shame. I thought even the things that no one knows, that somehow they read my mind."

12. What pain did longing for love cause you as a child? Or, what pain did you avoid by not longing for love? (Remember, it's always okay to answer "none.")

13. What pain has longing for love caused you within the past year? Or, what pain have you avoided by not longing for love?

> "I struggle with the idea that when someone is helping me I don't dare presume to think that I have something to offer them. . . . When it's there to hand them, some one slaps my hand and says, 'Who do you think you are to get up from your kneeling position?! Look how you wrecked things in your life.'"

"The fear involved in shame is of permanent abandonment, or exile. Those who see our reprehensible core will be so disgusted and sickened that we will be a leper and an outcast forever" (*The Wounded Heart*, page 72).

14. Do you identify with the fear of abandonment? If so, what are some of the things you do because of that fear?

15. As you look back over your answers in this chapter, think about who you are trusting. To what or whom have you given the power to determine your desirability and worth?

"I've been ashamed of my liking men because I always felt I was dirty."

16. Here are some ideas for ways to express your feelings about this chapter, especially if you're a visual person:

- Make a clay sculpture of how you see yourself, or as you think others see you. (See the box on page 59 of this workbook.)
- Make a collage about shame. It might be a picture of how you experience shame, or of the things that make you feel ashamed. Give it a title. Is there anyone you dare show it to?
- Go through collected photographs and select some that picture your feelings of shame. What makes them so shameful?
- Write how the collage "Shame" on page 65 of this workbook makes you feel. What thoughts does it evoke?

For Group Discussion

You may not want to tell your secrets to the other group members Here's a way to handle this session:

1. Check in with each other. How is each of you feeling right now? Can you explain in a few sentences what's going on with you, and perhaps why?

2. How easy was it for you to remember embarrassing things or how you felt about your body? Why do you think you find it easy or hard?

3. How easy was it for you to put your secrets and reasons into words (questions 5 and 6)? Why do you suppose that was so?

4. What are some things you learned about yourself from writing down all these shameful things?

5. Discuss what each of you has experienced when people have learned about your past abuse (question 7). How have those experiences affected you? What have you decided to keep doing or do differently when disclosing facts about your abuse?

6. Did you write mostly P's or G's beside your embarrassing moments and shameful truths (question 8)? What does that tell you about yourself?

7. You may be able to help each other with feedback on questions 9 and 10. What signs of deadening longings have you observed in each other?

8. You can keep your letter to God private or read parts of it aloud if you feel comfortable doing so (question 17). If some of you do decide to read parts of your letters, take time between readers to let the listeners tell how what they have heard makes them feel, or how they react to it.

9. How can members of your group support you today and this week as you deal with shame and trusting God in the midst of your current circumstances?

65

17. Write a letter to God, telling Him how you're feeling about what you've been writing in this chapter. Tell Him who or what you've been trusting, and how you feel about that. Tell Him what, if anything, you'd like to do differently and what, if anything, you'd like Him to do. Tell Him how you're feeling about Him.

If you feel mad at God today, that's okay—tell Him why. Tell Him why you don't trust Him, if you don't. Or tell Him why you'd rather get your longings met from somewhere else, or why you think He's not enough. In short, write whatever you really feel, even if you know it's "wrong" because it's unbiblical or unspiritual.

"Shame cannot exist with Light. Being known for what and who I am makes no room for shame. There's no need to hide in self-protection any longer. . . . Luke 7:36 and following—she's a *known* sinner. Shame cannot impact her. She has no pretense—she has found freedom for expressing her unique way to love her Lord. Her eyes are fixed only on Him—not on all that is around her."

CHAPTER SIX

CONTEMPT

Blinding Attack

Legitimate shame has the power to expose sin. It pierces the masquerade of idolatry and cuts open the heart to reveal a person's basis for life and hope. But we often find the light to be too bright and disturbing. Therefore, fallen man quickly resorts to a *shield* that seems to deflect the intrusion of God: the power of contempt. Contempt is absurd in that it inevitably increases our vulnerability even while it enables us to regain a semblance of control that blocks us from the humbling work of God.

Contempt is an attack against the perceived cause of shame. The shamed person wants to be invisible or too small to be noticed; hence, the eyes of the one who sees must be deflected or destroyed. There are two options. With self-contempt, the shamed one can turn her eyes away from the seer's stare and focus on the element of her being that has caused the shame. She counters the powerful emotion of shame with one of the few that is equally powerful: rage. Or, she can fasten contempt upon the seer, blinding his eyes with a hateful attack.

Contempt keeps all eyes safely away from our rebellion against God. Even when we whip ourselves for committing some sin, our goal is often to deflect attention away from our real crime: trying to be good and successful by ourselves without depending on God for anything. And if we punish ourselves, perhaps no one will notice that we haven't actually given up the sin at all.

Contempt says there is no one good enough to merit our trust—not even God. We have to handle the exposure of shame ourselves; we don't need God's forgiveness.

"Self-contempt . . . is Satan's counterfeit for conviction over sin. . . . A client told me about a fight with his wife. . . . He saw his problem as a failure of concentration, communication skills, and empathy. Those deficiencies do not get to the heart of his radical selfishness that protected him from responding to her rage. . . . His deep sense of failure did not touch his wife, nor give him the energy to move toward her. In fact, his contempt simply turned his eyes away from her, dulled his pain, explained why the marriage was so bad, and offered him a strategy to be nicer, but not more involved with his wife" (*The Wounded Heart*, page 88).

> "To be inwardly critical and want [my husband] to change serves to give me an excuse to be distanced from him. . . . Self-contempt gives me something to 'work on' rather than falling on the grace of God."

The Forms of Contempt

Read pages 77-89 of the book *The Wounded Heart*. Pages 80-83 sketch a progression of contempt from most to least severe. The next few questions will give you a chance to examine how you handle the shame of exposure. You'll also get a rough picture of how severe your self-contempt and other-centered contempt are. An S at the beginning of an item indicates self-contempt. An O indicates contempt for others. Some items could reflect contempt for self, others, or both; those items are marked SO.

1. Mark how often you think you do each of the following.

Least Severe Contempt

SO) I feel uncomfortable when someone compliments me.

never   rarely   sometimes   often   very often

SO) I feel uncomfortable when someone shows interest in me as a person.

never   rarely   sometimes   often   very often

SO) I feel uncomfortable when men pay attention to me.

never   rarely   sometimes   often   very often

SO) I feel uncomfortable when women pay attention to me.

never   rarely   sometimes   often   very often

I do these things mainly because I . . .

_____ S) feel unworthy of attention.
_____ O) don't trust people being kind or intimate.

O) I use humor to keep people pleased with me without getting close to the real me.

never   rarely   sometimes   often   very often

Other ways I keep people at a distance:

"I also display my contempt for others by trying to avoid them . . . although sometimes I'm not sure if this is really other-centered contempt or if it's just another symptom of my notion that I have nothing to offer."

Mildly Severe Contempt

S) I rebuke myself when I fail, make a mistake, or do something clumsy.

never   rarely   sometimes   often   very often

S) I beat up on myself when I sin.

never   rarely   sometimes   often   very often

O) I find fault with other people.

never   rarely   sometimes   often   very often

S) I tell myself I am ugly, fat, unattractive, unmasculine (if you're a man), or unfeminine (if you're a woman).

never   rarely   sometimes   often   very often

O) I am critical of people of the opposite sex.

never   rarely   sometimes   often   very often

SO) I am critical of people of the same sex.

never   rarely   sometimes   often   very often

O) I make fun of people of the opposite sex.

never   rarely   sometimes   often   very often

SO) I make fun of people of the same sex.

never   rarely   sometimes   often   very often

O) I am critical of my children.

never   rarely   sometimes   often   very often

O) At work, I get angry at subordinates, bosses, or peers when they make mistakes.

never   rarely   sometimes   often   very often

O) I feel I have to justify myself, giving excuses for my actions when challenged.

never   rarely   sometimes   often   very often

Other ways I measure my own or others' performance and push myself or others to perform better:

> "Contempt has helped me to remain safe, isolated—and miserable. I feel too ashamed and afraid to be vulnerable with very many people, so I pursue alienation with gusto."

Moderately Severe Contempt

S) if you're female; O) if you're male: I am sexually aroused by fantasies, descriptions, or depictions of women being abused or degraded.

never   rarely   sometimes   often   very often

S) if you're male; O) if you're female: I am sexually aroused by fantasies, descriptions, or depictions of men being abused or degraded.

never   rarely   sometimes   often   very often

S) I am sexually aroused by fantasies of myself being abused or degraded.

never   rarely   sometimes   often   very often

O) I daydream about revenge.

never   rarely   sometimes   often   very often

O) I enjoy violence in books, movies, etc.

never   rarely   sometimes   often   very often

S) I abuse food (vomiting, overeating, undereating, etc.), but not enough to threaten my life.

never   rarely   sometimes   often   very often

O) I'm willing to be dead emotionally as an act of revenge toward those I live with.

never   rarely   sometimes   often   very often

Other ways I desire, seek, or enjoy abuse of my own or another's personhood:

"For me, the obvious self-contempt was a struggle with weight. This was a slow self-destruction from a lifetime of bingeing. In essence, I was punishing the woman in me while at the same time daring others to come close past the layers of fat . . . and punishing my husband for his sins at the same time."

Very Severe Contempt

S) I think about suicide.

never   rarely   sometimes   often   very often

O) I think about killing someone else, or about that person dying.

never   rarely   sometimes   often   very often

S) I think about hurting myself physically.

never   rarely   sometimes   often   very often

S) I harm my body by cutting, scratching, etc.

never   rarely   sometimes   often   very often

O) I think about hurting someone else.

never   rarely   sometimes   often   very often

O) I hit my spouse, children, or others.

never   rarely   sometimes   often   very often

S) I try to get others to rape or hit me.

never   rarely   sometimes   often   very often

S) I endanger my life in risky or unsafe activities.

never   rarely   sometimes   often   very often

S) I do life-threatening things with food (vomiting, avoiding food, etc.).

never   rarely   sometimes   often   very often

Other ways I desire, seek, or enjoy my own or another's physical harm:

> "My relationships with men . . . were with men who took advantage of me—because I was so uncomfortable with men that really cared for me or liked me. I think, subconsciously, I believed that I deserved to be abused, used, treated badly, yelled at."

2. As you look over the signs of contempt you've found in your life, does it appear as though most of your contempt is directed toward yourself or toward others? (The inventory includes more O's than S's.)

3. Is your self-contempt mostly least to mildly severe? Moderate to very severe? Consistent from most to least? What about your contempt toward others? Mark where your answers tend to fall.

Self-contempt:

never	rarely	sometimes	often	very often

Contempt for others:

never	rarely	sometimes	often	very often

4. Given the pain in your life, it seems incomprehensible that in some ways you want contempt. At some level, your life feels better with contempt than without it. Why? Because contempt smothers that piercing ache of longing for what you don't have.

What happens when you treat yourself or others with contempt? What do you get out of it? (We'll address this further in the next section.)

> "Oddly, contempt has also served as my connection with feeling alive. As the contempt entices me to withdraw from people, I feel the intensity of the loneliness. The pain of isolation is not very pleasant. But to feel anything is at least some twisted reassurance that there is a glimmer of life in me."

5. Has going through the inventory increased your contempt for yourself or others? Given your personal tendencies toward contempt, what would you naturally do after completing questions 1 through 4?

6. What are you feeling right now . . .

   in your emotions?

   in your body?

7. What are you going to do?

8. If you're a visual person, try expressing one of the following through a collage or drawing:

   • My self-contempt looks/feels like . . .
   • My contempt for others looks/feels like . . .
   • I show my contempt by . . .
   • Right now I feel . . .

For Group Discussion

1. What did you think of the contempt inventory in question 1? How hard was it to complete? Did you find anything confusing? How did you feel during and after completing that inventory?

2. You probably don't want to compare individual answers to every item in the inventory. In addition to the other questions in this section, consider these:

   • What would you say are your two or three most common ways of treating yourself with contempt?
   • What are your favorite ways of treating others with contempt?
   • What did you learn about yourself from questions 1 through 3?

3. Does this section make you want to change anything about yourself? If so, what?

4. What did you do after completing this section? How did you feel?

Warning: Contempt is often the most intriguing concept people encounter in this process. It seems fun to identify all the ways we act contemptuous toward others, and they act toward us. But intrigue and understanding alone promote little change. It's essential that we let God lead us beyond understanding to sorrow over the ways we've hurt ourselves, others, and God through our contempt.

The Functions of Contempt

Diminishing Shame

"Shame always includes an aspect of anxiety. What will happen when I am found out? Will I be abandoned or mocked? . . . Contempt uses rage—sometimes loud and violent, and other times quiet and insidious—as a means of chasing away the uncertainty of shame. As long as contempt is present, shame will not stop a person in her tracks, but will energize action and movement away from the dreaded exposure" (*The Wounded Heart*, page 84).

9. Rage, even cold or polite rage, cancels out the anxiety we hate to feel. Do you see rage against yourself or others behind your contemptuous habits? If so, how?

> *Instead of feeling exposed, foolish, and laughable when I make a mistake, it's less painful for me to feel furious at myself. Other people may still be laughing at me, but at least I don't have to feel the humiliation because I'm busy feeling contempt for myself.*

> "My constant abrasiveness and impatience revealed a rage against people for not moving into my world."

10. How does your contempt protect you from the terror of rejection?

Deadening Longings

"In the midst of shame, longing for what the heart craves intensifies the anguish of the soul. . . . *For the woman or man who has been abused, one of the greatest enemies of the soul is the longing for intimacy.* . . . Contempt is a cruel anesthetic to longing. As long as I turn my condemnation against myself, I block the potential of your movement toward me and my longing for you to care. When I turn my condemnation against you, I am free from believing that I want anything from you. In either case, *contempt kills longing*" (*The Wounded Heart*, pages 84-85).

11. How does your contempt for yourself protect you from longing for someone to care?

> "My contempt for myself gave me all the excuse I needed to never admit I had needs and therefore to never have to experience real dependence on God. I never let anyone feel good about giving to me because I never took or I would take without showing serious need. It allowed me to have justification for keeping relationships distant."

12. How does your contempt for others protect you from longing for them to care?

If they're insensitive or uninteresting or too busy or not my kind of person, then I can tell myself it wouldn't be so great to have them want to be involved in my life.

Providing the Illusion of Control

"Fallen man works tenaciously, at times to psychotic lengths, to gain magical control over life by generating reasons that explain the why and what for of that which seems beyond his understanding. . . . This is particularly the case when the struggle involves deep personal loss. Why am I not married? Why did my husband leave me? Why did my father abuse me? . . . For many the raw reality of life in a fallen world is too much to endure; therefore, more acceptable, more controllable explanations must be found. . . .

"Consider the usefulness of self-contempt in dealing with a past of sexual abuse. One woman told me that as a five-year-old child she was apparently too sexy for her father to resist. . . . As long as she was at fault, she did not have to face her sorrow. Perhaps, even more, the explanation gave her a means of organizing and controlling her life. If she was abused because she was too sexy, all she need do is to hide any part of her body or spirit that men might find appealing. . . .

"*As long as I believe there is something I can do about my problem, then I am not constrained to feel hopeless.* A contemptuous explanation provides a direction to pursue to regain control over my emptiness" (*The Wounded Heart*, pages 85-87).

13. Is there anything you believe you did, or failed to do, to cause or encourage your abuse? What was it?

14. How have you tried to guard against ever making that mistake again?

"First, by blaming myself I was able to view my family as happy and healthy and to deny the overwhelming sadness, aloneness, and emptiness that was present in my home. Second, . . . as long as I remained the problem there was hope that there was something I could do to make my life happier. . . . It insulated me from having to admit my dependency upon Christ."

15. How easy is it for you to accept that you had absolutely no responsibility for or control over what happened to you? Why is that?

16. The main job of contempt is to deaden shame. If we feel we have some control over the problem, that there is something we can do about it, then we feel less naked and exposed. Think about your answer to question 14. How has pursuing that strategy made you feel a bit safer, a bit less naked?

> *If my big mistake was trusting a man, then by treating all men with contempt I can make myself safe from repeated abuse.*

Distorting the Real Problem

The fundamental goal of contempt is self-protection. Contempt achieves this by distorting the fact that the central human problem is sin.

Other-centered contempt ignores one's own depravity and centers the blame on another person's failure. It is Satan's counterfeit for loving rebuke. Other-centered contempt involves analysis for the aim of exploitation, feedback for the purpose of control. Likewise, as we said on page 67 of this guide, self-contempt is Satan's counterfeit for conviction over sin.

We've been hurt, terribly hurt. In our fallenness, our desires for love, intimacy, respect, attention, security, and a dozen others have become demands that we, others, and God give us what we want. When we, others, and God fail to grant or even hear those desires/demands, fierce rage begins to erupt in the deep places of our souls. It often never reaches the surface as volcanic violence and heat. Instead, it bubbles up and hardens as ice-cold rock that covers our hearts. Have our demands been rejected? Very well, *we* will reject our rejecters: self, others, and God. "I will not hurt!" we vow. "I will create for myself a better world, a better self, a better God!" we proclaim. The pronouncements of contempt may be shouted with fury, muttered cynically, or accompanied by a pleasant smile.

17. When you treat yourself with contempt, what are you hating yourself for?

Being passionate; being unmanly; being imperfect.

18. What do you do to protect yourself from being hurt? Write down as many habits and strategies as you can think of.

I trust no one.
I hide the real me behind a polite but bland mask.

"The contempt came back slowly but steadily in the form of disgusted sarcasm. 'So that's how quickly you let your defenses down. Only a month ago you wouldn't admit your need, steeled yourself against any kind words, were suspicious and angry at any sorrow or pity shown toward you—and now you have no shame. You're so desperate for any crumb of kindness you'll grovel for it. Who's going to want you when you're such an easy catch!'"

19. How does your contempt for others and yourself protect you from facing . . .

your longings and demands?

If I can just say, "The divorce was all my fault," then I don't have to hurt over how much I long for intimacy with a spouse or be deeply convicted about demanding that my husband treat me with kid gloves and give me my way.

the ways people have betrayed you?

If I can view my father as lower than a slug, then I don't have to feel the hurt and rejection and grief of his leaving us.

your loneliness?

If I'm lonely because I'm bad, then I can focus on rebuking my badness instead of aching over a loneliness I can't necessarily fix no matter what I do.

> "My self-contempt kept me hating myself and protected me from facing my anger and rage at others (especially for not coming through for me the way I longed for)."

20. Look back at the traits you checked in chapter 2. What do you think is the connection between the trait(s) you checked and contempt for yourself? What might you be getting out of those attitudes and behaviors that keeps you doing them even though you know you should stop? You can choose just three traits to examine.

For Group Discussion

Each participant should choose one of these statements, or any part of a statement, that reflects how he or she feels today or frequently. Then discuss what kind of contempt lies behind those chosen statements. How does that attitude hurt you and others? What do you get out of it that motivates you to do it?

____ I have known for a long time that I want to perfect being a zombie and numb myself to the memories. When it "works," I feel confident for a moment that the effect of my abuse was not as bad as the stories I have heard and read about other abuse victims.

____ I really do think I'm trying to punish myself. If I do that, then none of those other things (having an accident or being in a tragic catastrophe) will happen to me. It's a strange feeling, a physical feeling. It's almost like I know I'm hurting myself, my body can feel it, but I deny that feeling.

____ I have no rights. I have to please other people.

____ I have withdrawn in the last few years. I can't understand what I'm afraid of. If it were physical danger, like the fear of dying, I could understand. I have this great unbelievable fear of people not liking me the way I am. I'm not good enough; people won't like me.

____ I cut myself off. The good things in life are not for me. As long as I remain so far away from being an acceptable or accepting compatriot with people in the world, I might as well stay on my island. I made myself into this phantom, something so out of touch and out of tune with the rest of the world that I needed to keep isolated on an island.

____ I start to feel a terror, like a huge black cloud that creeps up. My thoughts start to race so fast I don't know what they are. Then I go for food, shopping, television, or any other pleasure that can distract me. Even though I may rush through my food or feel unsettled as I scurry to find relief, it is better than the terror.

____ Whatever I do, it will never be enough. I know I am smart; I know I have a lot of skills. If I say I'll do a job, I have no doubt that it will get done, and probably in half the time it would take anyone else. My problem is, I don't feel I deserve anything for it. Everything I do, great as it is, is only making up for what happened when I was a child. My achievement can only bring me up to zero.

For Men Only

21. How does your contempt show itself with other men? Is that contempt different from the contempt you feel for women?

22. What do you do when you lose an athletic contest, or look at the checkbook at the end of the month, or fail in a business-related decision?

****

We are rarely able to endure legitimate shame, the shame over sin. We tend to transfer the sorrow for hurting someone to violence or addictions. The deadness of contempt smothers life-giving sorrow. Contempt is powerful and energizing, yet there will always be a hollowness behind the eyes of the furiously violent or furiously addicted person.

23. The bridge out of contempt is a *willingness to choose sorrow* over violence or addiction. Whom has your contempt harmed? Do you sense any sorrow in yourself for that harm?

Even if I caused you sorrow by my letter, I do not regret it. Though I did regret it—I see that my letter hurt you, but only for a little while—yet now I am happy, not because you were made sorry, but because your sorrow led you to repentance. For you became sorrowful as God intended and so were not harmed in any way by us. Godly sorrow brings repentance that leads to salvation and leaves no regret, but worldly sorrow [shame/contempt] brings death. See what this godly sorrow has produced in you: what earnestness, what eagerness to clear yourselves, what indignation, what alarm, what longing, what concern, what readiness to see justice done. (2 Corinthians 7:8-11)

24. a. How do you feel right now? What sensations are you aware of in your body (nausea, numbness, tightness, hunger, shaking, calmness)?

b. What would you normally do to escape or deal with what you are feeling?

25. How do you feel about God right now? What would you like Him to do or not do?

For Group Discussion
1. What was hard or confusing about this section?
2. What did you learn about your personal reasons for your contempt?
3. What does looking at those reasons make you feel? Consider the following.
•Helpless
•Frustrated
•Humble before God
•Desperately wanting to find ways to change
•Contempt for yourself for being such a sinner
4. How are you feeling about God right now? Why?
5. What help would you like from God in dealing with your contempt?
6. How could other group members help you?

CHAPTER SEVEN

POWERLESSNESS

Facing the Damage

What does abuse do to a person's soul? It is as though God had planted a garden that in time would yield a rich crop of faith, hope, and love, but a vicious someone has driven a herd of pigs through the garden to trample the seedlings, and then has sown weeds in their place. Those weeds that mock the intended crop are powerlessness, betrayal, and ambivalence.

In this chapter and the next two, you will have a chance to examine how you have experienced the damage of powerlessness, ambivalence, and betrayal. But first, an obvious question arises. What is the point of looking at damage through a microscope? When someone has cancer, the surgeon cuts the tumor out while the patient sleeps. The patient never has to see the tumor, study photos of diseased flesh, or even read lab reports. One does not heal better from cancer by studying the damage it has caused.

Cancer of the soul is different. If the enemy is denial, the stubborn commitment to redraw God and our world in colors we prefer, then honesty—truth—is a powerful weapon. The danger of not truly facing the damage is that the deep infection will never be reached and cut out. Then we become like the spiritual leaders God condemned through the prophet Jeremiah:

> "They dress the wound of my people
>   as though it were not serious.
> 'Peace, peace,' they say,
>   when there is no peace."
>   (Jeremiah 6:14)

But there is also danger in facing the damage. Under the microscope it may seem even larger than it is, too large to heal, if we fail to keep in view the great skill of our Surgeon. Our feelings seem numb and our memories are sketchy, precisely because the pain of the damage overwhelms us. The title of Jamie Buckingham's book is accurate: *The Truth Will Set You Free, But First It Will Make You Miserable*. It won't be pleasant to look at the ugly truth under bright light.

"True hope never minimizes a problem in order to make it more palatable and easily managed. For the Christian, hope begins by recognizing the utter hopelessness of our condition and the necessity of divine intervention, if we are to experience true joy. Any personal change that can be achieved solely through human, in contrast to supernatural, intervention will neither satisfy nor change our heart. A proper focus on the deep wound is therefore neither negative nor does it promote despair. Rather, it sets the stage for the dramatic work of God" (*The Wounded Heart*, page 113).

A second danger is that by looking too long at one kind of damage, we may begin to imagine it more serious than, or independent of, other kinds. We are distinguishing powerlessness from betrayal and ambivalence only to make it easier to think and talk about, not because it ever really operates independently.

The magnitude of the damage may even encourage us to see ourselves only as victims, not as people who can choose a better path now. We may begin to feel we have a right to do whatever we have to do to protect ourselves from further hurt, that our terrible wounds exempt us from the responsibility to love God and others in risky ways. But the truth is, we are not powerless as long as the Spirit of God lives inside us, ever willing to empower wise and loving choices. Nor are we exempt from loving just because we have been cruelly unloved. We are not free to pass abuse on to the next victim.

One danger is the most subtle. It is possible to face the damage with the conviction that the damage, rather than our strategies for avoiding pain, is the problem. We feel the damage so intensely, but we are often numb to the ways we fail to love ourselves, others, and God as we should. We go through our days determined to make life work without God, blind to our outrageous arrogance. Thus, facing the damage is a crucial step in the process, but it will not bring about change on its own. If we face our damage but ignore our arrogance, we will simply become angrier, more determined to do whatever it takes not to be hurt again. This commitment to self-protection will make it impossible for us to truly love.

Stripped of Choice

One of the most precious gifts God has placed in the human soul is the ability to choose. He who had all power to decide everything did not want a race of robots, so He yielded to men and women the freedom to make choices that matter. A human will can say, "I choose this," and God rarely prevents the consequences. He exercises control over a human will only to the degree that that will is voluntarily submitted to Him.

Our freedom to choose is narrowly limited; we often find there is nothing we can do to affect a situation. But abuse cuts deeper than the ordinary frustrations of life. It strips a person of the God-given freedom to choose in the areas that matter most to him or her.

Whether our abuse occurred one time or hundreds, we were never really free to choose for or against it. We were powerless in three ways:

- We were helpless to turn our families into places of warm, nourishing relationships.
- We had no true power to stop the abuse itself from happening; our abuser made sure that avenues of escape were blocked.
- We were and still are helpless to end the relentless pain in our soul.

In the next three sections we'll examine each wellspring of powerlessness. As you answer the questions, try to be open to feeling whatever comes up. Often, part of our denial is locking the sense of helpless desperation and terror in a strong trunk so it won't drive us mad. Part of allowing God to take over the job of protecting us from madness is handing Him the key to this trunk.

We tend to resist the idea that we were powerless because it seems so horrible to see ourselves as helpless victims. Children think they are the center of the universe and that they have power to affect all sorts of things. Before you explore your powerlessness, try to recall the things you have felt responsible for.

1. Complete this sentence at least twice: If I had (hadn't) . . . , my parents (or guardians) would (not) have . . . .

> *If I hadn't rebelled in high school, my parents would have paid for me to*
> *attend college.*
> *If I hadn't been abused, my parents would still be married.*

The Empty Home

Read pages 113-116 of *The Wounded Heart*. Also, reread what you wrote in questions 1 through 3 of chapter 4, pages 44-46 of this guide.

2. What would you say was missing from your relationship with your father that made you vulnerable to abuse? In what ways did he fail to protect you from harm or provide warm intimacy for you? (It's okay to answer "nothing" if that's what you really think.)

3. What was missing from your relationship with your mother? How did she neglect you emotionally or fail to protect you?

4. When you have visited other families, as a child or an adult, what good things have you observed that were absent from your home?

5. What did you do to try to fix the problems in your home?

> "When my parents would start arguing over something stupid at dinner, my brother would immediately get up and leave the table. But I would stay and try to play arbitrator—'I think what she's trying to say is . . . .'"

6. How did you respond when you failed to fix the problems?

The Helplessness of Abuse

Read pages 116-117 of *The Wounded Heart*.

7. Review the rest of your answers in chapter 4. What factors made you helpless to stop the assault, even if you were not physically forced? How were you denied real options, time to reflect, adult perspective on the issues involved, or opportunity to consult with someone with perspective? How were you coerced or shamed into submission? (You may not have answers for all five.)

I had no real options because . . .

> *No one would have kept him from hurting me if I had told.*
> *My mother would have had a nervous breakdown if she'd known.*
> *The whole family would have exploded apart.*
> *No one would have believed me.*

I had no time to reflect because . . .

> *My abuser would start touching me out of the blue, and I was always startled and confused.*

I lacked adult perspective because . . .

> *I was only ten. People don't get the ability to detect deceit and reason out alternatives until they reach puberty.*
> *I didn't know anything about sex or what it meant.*

I couldn't consult with anybody because . . .

I was coerced or shamed by . . .

8. Do you remember feeling helpless at the time? Describe what you remember, if anything.

> "It never occurred to me to try to stop him. I was obviously no match for him. But it got boring for him when I just lay there like a plastic dummy, so he invented a game: 'Pretend you're being raped and struggle to get away.' I felt far more horribly helpless when I struggled and was overpowered than when I just gave in."

9. How do you feel now when you think about how helpless you were?

The Bleeding Soul

Read pages 117-118 of *The Wounded Heart.*

10. How have you tried to relieve or deaden the pain of being abused and not being deeply loved?

For Group Discussion

Some of you may find it hard to see how you were truly helpless to prevent your abuse. You may feel there must be something you could have done, or you may scold yourself for not doing what you now know you should have done. It can be terrifying to face the fact that you were completely helpless. Let the group help you past self-contempt and denial. Describe the situation you faced. Tell what you think you should have done, if you believe you know. Tell how old you were. What do group members think? Did you have real options, given the state of your family and what a child of that age is capable of?

11. What signs do you see in your life that you have been unable to completely deaden the pain?

> "For me, to never be found inadequate is to never be found powerless or lacking as a man. I was too powerless to make wise decisions at the time of the abuse. One way I protect from being put in that position again is to try to seek knowledge. Knowledge becomes a way to avoid the loss of control in future events."

12. How do you feel when you think about having failed to escape your pain, no matter what you've done?

What Has Powerlessness Done in Me?

In this chapter and the next two, we'll look at the effects of powerlessness, ambivalence, and betrayal from two angles. On one hand, how has each of these affected what happens *inside us*: our thoughts, feelings, beliefs, inner commitments? And on the other hand, how have these affected what we *do:* how we treat ourselves, others, and God?

What we think and what we do are so closely intertwined that it would be hard to talk about them entirely separately. So, we'll explore them together, then afterward you'll have a chance to summarize what you've learned about what's inside you and what you do. Honestly facing what you do will carry you a long way in the process of change.

For Group Discussion

When you've explored the different strands of powerlessness, step back and consider powerlessness in general. Have you felt powerless since you started thinking about it? Discuss how it feels, what it makes you feel like doing, how it affects the rest of your life.

Oddly enough, many of us felt like the key member of our families—what we did determined how things went—even while feeling powerless to fix the family's problems. It was especially frustrating to feel both responsible and helpless. Question 1 attempts to get at this contradiction. If that's true of you, talk about how it felt to be the kingpin or cornerstone of your family. Does your family still make you responsible for how things go or how others feel? How does that interact with powerlessness?

So, what about powerlessness? When our efforts to fix our families failed, we were forced to slowly face the fact that we would never be good, smart, talented, or competent enough to make things right. Few of us concluded from this fact that fixing our families was never our responsibility. Instead, deep, contemptuous *self-doubt* began to nag at us. "Why can't I run faster or sing better or be more perfect? There must be something wrong with me."

Self-doubt invited *despair.* When we continually tried and failed to escape abuse and pain, we decided to abandon hope of escape. Self-doubt said, "There must be something I can do." Despair whispered a hideous dissent: "There is nothing I can do (and no one else will intervene)." We still shift back and forth among them through depression, the unhappy medium.

The only way to survive despair was by *deadening* the parts of our soul that still felt rage, pain, and desire: "I will not hope, I will not feel, I will not respond to this ugliness." We faced a grim choice, since the only way to be pain free is to be dead. We weren't entirely successful at deadening ourselves, but we still suffer the effects of our partial success.

Doubt, despair, and deadness are core attitudes and commitments that affect nearly everything we do. Read pages 118-120 of *The Wounded Heart.*

13. Your self-doubt, despair (or depression), and deadness may or may not be immediately obvious to you. How would you rewrite these sentences to fit your situation?

Self-Doubt
What is wrong with me that I can't do this . . . well enough to change this . . . ?

Despair
There's no hope in even trying to . . . anymore. It's hopeless.

Deadness
If I don't feel . . . , then . . . .

14. How would you summarize the way you've responded to feeling powerless? What did you learn about yourself from question 13?

> "I have had a recurring nightmare that I live in a huge house and every room looks like an antique shop, and it takes me all night to go through one room to clean it up. My married children and two toddlers have lived with us for a year and a half. . . . Powerless to have my home the way I want it has been God's way of dealing with my issues. . . . The need to 'get it done' invades my thought life. . . .
>
> "The feeling of powerlessness and panic also comes when I feel pinned down sexually. I want to be free to move or I feel like it is rape."

What happens to us when doubt, despair, and deadness rule our soul? Deep helplessness usually leads to a lifestyle marred by the *loss of our sense of pain*. That loss makes us *lose our sense of self*, which in turn *impairs our judgment* and wisdom about relationships. The result is often tragic.

Read pages 120-126 of *The Wounded Heart*.

Loss of a Sense of Pain

15. Which, if any, of these sounds like you?

____ I have a very high tolerance for physical pain. I tend not to notice when I'm sick or injured.

> "The feeling of being powerless prompted me to be responsible for others and other things that I was not responsible for, thus creating an unhealthy sense of boundaries, or no boundaries at all."

____ When I feel physical pain, I try to ignore it.

____ I have trouble feeling anything in my body.

____ I have trouble feeling emotions.

____ I remember few specific painful memories of my past.

____ I feel like Dr. Jekyll and Mr. Hyde. Often I'm an obedient Christian, but I have an immoral side that erupts from time to time. I hate what I do when I'm Mr. Hyde, and I try to keep it secret, but I can't seem to stop it.

____ I can't remember the last time I did something really bad.

16. a. Do you feel as though you have a "good" side and a "bad" side? If you do, what is your "good" side like? What does it do?

b. What is your "bad" side like? What does it do?

Loss of a Sense of Self

Feelings of emotional and physical longings, pleasure, and pain are what let us know we're alive. When we deaden our longings and our ability to feel pain, we lose a sense of being who we really are.

17. Do you ever feel as though there's no one home in your soul, that you are somewhere else? Describe that feeling.

> "I have nearly perfected the art of being so lost in my work that I can circumvent virtually all feeling—for a time."

For some of us, our past seems too shameful to admit to others—or even to ourselves. Some of us fear what people (including us) will think of us if they find out the kind of family we come from, so we may concoct a history that sounds like the perfect childhood. Others of us want the attention caring people give to abuse victims, but the reality of what we've suffered seems too agonizing to face. In that case, we may invent a tale of an abusive childhood that differs enough from reality to let us receive the attention without suffering the pain.

18. Consider the roles that fantasy, pretending, or lying have in your life.

    a. What stories have you made up about your past?

    b. What kinds of fantasies about your present or future do you have fairly often?

    c. What other role does pretending or lying have in your life, if any?

Loss of Judgment

When we deaden our senses to pain, to longings, to our past and identity, we cut ourselves off from some of the crucial resources we need for making decisions. Our warning buzzer that tells us "this person/thing is dangerous" goes off at the wrong time and then fails to sound when it should. We don't hear our longings tell us "this is what I long for," so we continually fail to choose what would be most nourishing for us. We lack the wisdom that comes from experience because we have suppressed or rewritten our experiences. Hence, while we may make brilliant decisions about work or practical matters, we are over and over incredibly foolish regarding relationships.

> "At work I'm fantastic. Everyone thinks I walk on water. I feel competent and together—I *am* competent and together! Is it any wonder that I'd rather be at work than doing things with people, where I'm constantly making dumb mistakes? How can I be so sharp about business and so stupid about relationships?"

19. Do you have trouble hearing or trusting your intuitions about relationships? If so, what's that like? What happens?

One root of poor judgment is shame: "I'm not worthy to be in relationship with a truly loving man." The other root is contempt for self and others. The man capable of deep relationship is more dangerous; abandonment by him will hurt far more than abandonment by an uncommitted man. The good man is also far harder to control, and we hate feeling powerless to control someone. For both of these reasons, we often opt for those who are incapable of deep relationship.

> "So, so much of my style of relating came in response to a fierce determination to not be powerless in the world outside my home—and that was also fueled by being very successful and gifted. . . When overt sexual harassment and abuse in the interactive category entered my workplace and began escalating, and I began experiencing those feelings of powerlessness, fear, and rage that I had felt as an abused little girl inside my home, I think that was a very crucial turning point in my recovery, even though it was to be over a year before I had memories of overt sexual abuse in my past surface."

20. Do your relationships reflect any of these traits?

_____ I have a pattern of being the victim in relationships.

_____ I have to be in control.

_____ I prefer to be around people less clever than I am.

_____ I usually feel controlled by the other person.

_____ I tend to hold the core of myself aloof from others.

_____ It's as though there's a chasm or glass wall separating me from those around me.

_____ I feel unable to make myself understood.

_____ Because I know I'm no good at relationships, I tend to be uptight when I have to deal with one.

_____ Because I know I'm no good at relationships, I avoid them.

For Women Only
21. Which of these (if any) describe the kind of man you are now involved with or often have been involved with?

_____ He can't make decisions.

_____ He defends his weaknesses with distance that occasionally erupts in rage.

_____ He's too busy to be deeply involved in relationship with me.

_____ He's detached from both his work and me.

_____ He doesn't want intimacy.

_____ He's untrustworthy.

_____ He's too dead to do anything dangerous.

_____ He shows no passion.

_____ He uses emotion (anger, lust, fear, guilt) to control me.

> "When I am in situations now when I am powerless, rather than living my life to avoid it, or being oblivious to it, I am more aware of it. I don't as often respond by toughening up and trying harder. I am more inclined to realize the pain and confusion of being powerless, and to look to and anticipate the return of the all-powerful One, and to know that He will ultimately prevail."

****

For Men Only
22. Which of these (if any) describe the kind of woman you are now involved with or often have been involved with?

_____ She is dominating.

_____ She is unwilling to express what she wants or feels.

_____ She sends mixed signals about intimacy.

_____ She is too busy to be deeply involved with me.

_____ She seems to invite misuse.

_____ She is untrustworthy.

_____ She gets angry enough to intimidate me.

_____ She seems to feel nothing when I want her to feel something.

_____ She uses emotions (anger, lust, fear, guilt) to control me.

23. Do any of these sound like the way you tend to think deep down?

_____ I'm not good enough to be involved with a truly loving man/woman. A really wonderful man/woman would never want me.

_____ It's more important to me to be in control of a relationship than to have it be deep and intimate.

_____ If I had a terrific man/woman and lost him/her, it would be far worse than never having him/her.

24. Step back and look at these attitudes. What do you think of them? What do you like? What do you not like?

In Summary

25. Look back over your responses to questions 13 through 24. Overall, how would you say experiencing powerlessness has affected your *inner self*—your attitudes, feelings, and commitments?

26. What would you say are the top few ways in which feeling powerless has affected the ways you treat yourself and others?

YOURSELF

OTHERS

****

For Men Only

Men often handle their sense of powerlessness by gaining a rock-solid control over their emotions. Many men are exceptionally proud of feeling "nothing." When others would feel anger or fear, these men feel calm, cool, and in control. Many men feel good when they are above normal human realities, such as joy, sadness, loneliness, and longing. We must learn to acknowledge that no moment goes by without some inner awareness or feeling; it is the way God made us. Further, we must accept that no emotion is unmanly.

A second mode of reasserting control in the midst of powerlessness for many men is physical or sports prowess. A strong body asserts mastery and power. A deep absorption in sports gives a sense of boldness, courage, and control in an activity that resembles bloodless warfare.

Another manner of gaining power is through sexual exploitation. Men are apt to use sex for more than pleasure or intimacy; sexuality is often an overt or subtle means of "making someone pay." This can be accomplished through a casual affair, fantasies of domination or subjugation, sexual abuse, sexual harassment, or seductive behavior.

27. a. How do you use emotional distance, coldness, or control to assert power and block others from infringing on your heart?

b. How do you use exercise, sports, or physical strength (or its absence) to gain back the ground lost in past abuse?

c. In what ways do you make women or other men pay through the misuse of your sexuality?

****

For Group Discussion

If you prefer not to wade through this section question by question, focus on questions 25, 26, and 28.

28. Think of a situation in which you currently feel helpless in some way. Set a timer for twenty minutes, and write about that situation—whatever comes to mind. For instance, what's making you feel helpless? What is the feeling like? What would you normally do in a situation like this? What would normally happen if you did that? What would you like to be able to do instead? What do you think would happen if you did that? You can write your thoughts on this page and the next, or you can write them in your own journal notebook.

Continue journal writing on this page.

29. Here are some ideas for visual people:

- Paint, draw, or sculpt yourself as a child in a way that depicts your helplessness at that age.
- Photograph some children who are at the age you were when you were abused. Do they look powerful or vulnerable? How does it feel for you to look at them?
- Make a collage or painting that depicts the feeling of powerlessness.

30. How are you feeling right now? What do you feel like doing?

Does God Understand Powerlessness?

We've looked at inner attitudes and outer actions toward ourselves and others. What about God? How has powerlessness moved us to view and treat God?

The LORD is my rock, my fortress and my deliverer;
  my God is my rock, in whom I take refuge. . . .
He rescued me from my powerful enemy,
  from my foes, who were too strong for me.
They confronted me in the day of my disaster,
  but the LORD was my support. (Psalm 18:2, 17-18)

Who can speak and have it happen
  if the Lord has not decreed it?
Is it not from the mouth of the Most High
  that both calamities and good things come?
    (Lamentations 3:37-38)

> "I felt so trapped by God because I knew He held all the power. I believed in God's power to grant longings, but struggled with the question of *would* He, not *could* He. I've kept God in the abuser role. I did not want Him to be as good as He is because it requires too much from me. It is much easier to keep Him in the abuser role and hate Him."

The Bible asserts that God has all power to do whatever He wants. From one point of view that's great news. But the catch is that in the day of our disaster, God allowed our powerful enemy to abuse us unchallenged. How are we to trust a God who permits calamities, who very often allows the most vicious acts of abuse?

When we feel powerless, the Bible's comfort is that God has all power. We can't protect ourselves, but God can. We can't heal ourselves, but God can. What, then, are we to do when He doesn't?

We blame ourselves: "I didn't know Jesus when I was seven. I didn't ask Him to help me, so He didn't." We blame God: "God must be a sadist who likes to see children suffer." Or, "Maybe He didn't take care of me because He was busy with things and people more important to Him than I was. Perhaps the pain of one human was insignificant to Him in His pursuit of lofty plans." We come up with a reasonable reason: "God is going to use my suffering for some good purpose. It will make me more loving. It will show how wonderful He is when I'm better. I'll find out it was worth it when I get to heaven."

None of these approaches will get us anywhere if we use it as a neat explanation to dispose of the problem so we can get on with life. Any explanation that leads us away from struggling with God is ultimately unhelpful. Conversely, almost any honest question—even a hurt or angry one—that pursues God Himself to come near and reveal Himself will probably be helpful in the long run. An honest wrestler will get further with God than someone who has God figured out.

"As the heavens are higher than the earth,
*   so are my ways higher than your ways*
*   and my thoughts than your thoughts." (Isaiah 55:9)*

Though he brings grief, he will show compassion,
*   so great is his unfailing love.*
For he does not willingly bring affliction
*   or grief to the children of men. (Lamentations 3:32-33)*

31. How do you usually treat God when you are feeling helpless about a situation?

32. Look at your answers to questions 26 through 29. What attitudes about God do they reflect?

When we were starving for our families' love, and yet faced cruelty daily, God seemed absent. Was He powerless to intervene? No. We may not be able to explain fully why He didn't, but we can rule out some possibilities. We know it's not because He doesn't care about us, enjoys to see us suffering, was angry at us, or was too busy.

Jesus' sacrifice on the cross debunks all these suspicions. We know God understands and cares about human powerlessness intimately because Jesus, who is God, endured the most severe loss of power ever. First He emptied Himself of His divine safety and His limitless ability to do anything and be everywhere. He became not just human, but the baby of a poor teenager. For us who have never experienced absolute power, it's hard to imagine what it might be like to have always experienced it and then to give it up to become human.

Jesus accepted the ordinary powerlessness of being human in a fallen world. But He went further to subject Himself to the helplessness of abuse, even to the point of not even having His Father to lean on.

Then the governor's soldiers took Jesus into the Praetorium and gathered the whole company of soldiers around him. They stripped him and put a scarlet robe on him, and ten twisted together a crown of thorns and set it on his head. They put a staff in his right hand and knelt in front of him and mocked him. "Hail, king of the Jews!" they said. They spit on him, and took the staff and struck him on the head again and again. . . .

When they had crucified him, they divided up his clothes by casting lots. . . .

Those who passed by hurled insults at him, shaking their heads and saying, "You who are going to destroy the temple and build it in three days, save yourself! Come down from the cross, if you are the Son of God!"

In the same way the chief priests, the teachers of the law and the elders mocked him. "He saved others," they said, "but he can't save himself! He's the King of Israel! Let him come down now from the cross, and we will believe in him. He trusts in God. Let God rescue him now if he wants him, for he said, 'I am the Son of God.'" In the same way the robbers who were crucified with him also heaped insults on him. . . .

About the ninth hour Jesus cried out in a loud voice, "Eloi, Eloi, lama sabachthani?"—which means, "My God, my God, why have you forsaken me?" (Matthew 27:27-30,35,39-44,46)

God understands the anguish of powerlessness. Oddly enough, His choice to endure the helplessness of humanness and death was a loving response to our freely chosen commitment to live life without Him. And we are free to choose for or against Him only because He gave us the power to make that choice. God chose not to supernaturally defend us against our abusers so that those abusers could have the genuine freedom He granted to all humans: the freedom to choose good or evil. We, in turn, have the freedom to choose to abuse or love the people around us.

Jesus knew that the Roman governor Pilate was responsible before God for his choice to have Jesus executed. At the same time He was confident that His Father was in charge.

Pilate said, "Don't you realize I have power either to free you or to crucify you?"

Jesus answered, "You would have no power over me if it were not given to you from above." (John 19:10-11)

33. Does it make any difference to you that Jesus endured such abuse for your sake? How are you feeling about God now?

34. The Cross was what God decided to do about the abusers in the world. If you were God, what would you do about the abusers in the world?

35. As you think back over this chapter on powerlessness, what do you feel like doing?

36. Is there anything you'd like to say to God now? If there is, write it down.

CHAPTER EIGHT

AMBIVALENCE

"Ambivalence can be defined as *feeling two contradictory emotions at the same moment*. . . . An experience of relational pleasure (being invited to go fishing or being complimented about personal attractiveness) or sensual pleasure (being hugged) or sexual pleasure (being touched on the primary or secondary sexual parts) will arouse deep parts of the soul. Sexual pleasure in particular is both frightening and stimulating to a young child. . . . When the same pleasure is connected with the experience of being powerless, betrayed, and used, then untold damage will occur. . . . The inevitable feelings of both enjoyment and shame produce the anguish of ambivalence. *Central to understanding ambivalence is the fact that the very thing that was despised also brought some degree of pleasure*" (*The Wounded Heart*, pages 143,146).

This is a horrible idea. Especially if we were physically harmed, but even if we weren't, it is revolting to think we felt anything but terror, pain, fury, and shame during our abuse. The suggestion that we might have had mixed feelings seems to support the disgusting lie that we at least partly wanted what happened.

But it does not imply that. It is completely possible that our bodies reacted the way bodies are supposed to react to touch, or that as perverse as our abuser's attention was, it was better than the emotional wasteland we felt in our homes. For some of us, it's great news that the orgasm we felt or the comic book we accepted doesn't prove we asked for the abuse. But for others of us who were perhaps painfully raped, it's hard to imagine we could have felt even the slightest flicker of pleasure at having some power over this person. Yet that flicker, now hidden away, is the root of much of the shame and craziness that pursues us through life.

Because of our abuse, most of us struggle with mixed feelings about sex, being feminine or masculine, being attractive or unattractive, being friends or lovers. We hate the memories and images that come uninvited to our minds, yet they have a macabre fascination for us, like gripping horror films. We can't shed the feeling that somehow we *must* be partly responsible for the abuse. All of these are shadows of ambivalence.

Read pages 143-156 of *The Wounded Heart*.

The Past

1. Ambivalence comes in many flavors. Check the statements that apply to you. Complete unfinished sentences.

____ I remember terrible physical pain.

____ I remember feeling terror.

____ I remember feeling shame.

____ I remember feeling betrayed.

____ I remember feeling used.

____ I remember feeling confused.

____ I remember feeling . . .

____ I felt pleasure in the way my abuser related to me before, during, or after the abuse. The part I enjoyed was . . .

> "It was as if I could distinctly separate myself into two separate identities—the one who looked together physically, mentally, and spiritually, and the one who held and struggled with dark secrets forever locked inside my own wounded heart."

____ I enjoyed the attention.

____ I enjoyed the nonsexual touching.

____ I felt sexually aroused.

____ I had an orgasm.

____ I enjoyed the feeling of power over someone.

____ I enjoyed feeling like I was attractive.

____ I don't remember enjoying anything.

____ I'm sure I didn't enjoy anything.

____ I don't remember what happened.

2. Imagine you are being tried in court. The prosecutor (in Hebrew he would be the *satan* [accuser]) is accusing you of being at least partly responsible for your abuse. What evidence would he raise? What secret nagging accusations plague you? What might your abuser say to shift the blame to you?

Complete the following sentence as many times as you can. Don't stop to evaluate whether the reasons you are writing are good or bad. Just get them all on paper.

I must be at least partly responsible for the abuse because . . .

> *I never said no.*
> *I let him cuddle me.*
> *I took the presents.*
> *I had an erection.*

I must be at least partly responsible for the abuse because . . .

I must be at least partly responsible for the abuse because . . .

I must be at least partly responsible for the abuse because . . .

I must be at least partly responsible for the abuse because . . .

3. Now call in your defense attorney (1 John 2:1). How could he refute each accusation? If you need to, go back over what you've read in *The Wounded Heart*, looking for answers. Reread your answers to question 7 of chapter 7 in this guide (page 88). Ask a friend or a counselor to help you. Don't give up until you clearly understand why none of the prosecutor's reasons are valid.

I wasn't responsible because. . . .

> *I was afraid to say no.*
> *I was starved for attention, and it's not wrong for a child to enjoy cuddling.*
> *Asking for cuddling wasn't the same as asking for sex.*

I wasn't responsible because . . .

I wasn't responsible because . . .

I wasn't responsible because . . .

I wasn't responsible because . . .

"For the first time in my life, someone (my abuser) had shown me some sense of 'gentle,' positive attention. I really couldn't put words to what he was doing to me, but it felt wonderful and horrible at the same time. Part of me enjoyed the experience, and I felt so wicked for taking pleasure in it that I figured I deserved whatever bad consequences would befall me. Maybe if I minimized the damage I could minimize the punishment, too."

I wasn't responsible because . . .

The Present

4. Things that happen to us in the present also stir those confused, ambivalent feelings. Even today, we sometimes seem to find pleasure in something horrible. Check the sentences that apply to you.

109

_____ I have nightmares of my abuse.

_____ I have dreams of my abuse that arouse me sexually.

_____ I have sudden memories of my abuse or abuser while I'm awake.

_____ I partly enjoy and partly hate having memories of abuse.

_____ As horrible as the memories are, they somehow fascinate me.

_____ I tend to have memories when I . . .

    _____ feel stressed.

    _____ am about to succeed.

    _____ am about to fail.

    _____ am having sex.

    _____ Other (name it):

_____ When I relate to my abuser today, I'm partly drawn and partly repulsed.

_____ I become sexually aroused only when I remember or imagine being abused.

_____ I feel sexually aroused when a man/woman is kind to me.

_____ I feel vulnerable and afraid when someone is kind to me.

5. Memories, or not being able to remember, make me feel . . .

_____ on edge all the time.

_____ out of control.

_____ frustrated.

_____ terrified.

_____ confused.

_____ like I'm making progress.

_____ alive.

> "I try to go with what will please and appease, and then hate myself for doing it. I change my mind, and people experience me as undependable."

_____ relieved.

_____ nothing.

_____ Other (name it):

The Future

Perhaps the most discouraging part of our situation is that we seem to relive our abuse over and over. The future seems doomed to repeat the past; because, as much as we hate what happens, in some queer way we are getting something out of it. What that something *is* usually isn't obvious.

6. Obvious revictimization is being sexually assaulted or abused again. More subtle revictimization is repeating a scenario or a way of relating over and over.

Do you find patterns repeating themselves in your relationships? Even if you don't see any clear connection between those patterns and your abuse, describe the patterns you see.

> *I've been raped three times by men I was dating.*
> *I seem to be drawn to men who are angry and controlling.*
> *I'm always falling for fragile, overly dependent women.*
> *It seems like just when I start to feel I'm good friends with a man, he either makes a sexual advance or runs away.*

7. How does it make you feel to see these threads of ambivalence in your life?

What Has Ambivalence Done in Me?

Questions 8 through 18 will help you identify some of the ways ambivalence has affected you. Connecting the weeds with the root should prepare you to begin pulling them out.

Shame and Contempt

Ambivalence floods us with shame and contempt. It feels disgusting to think we felt even the tiniest bit of pleasure in our abuse. We get furious with ourselves when we get into the same type of sick relationship over and over.

Confusion deepens our shame. How could I feel arousal and hatred at the same moment? Why do I feel sexually aroused when someone is kind to me? It doesn't help when people react to those questions with shock, disgust, or condemnation. The only thing that seems to kill the shame is contempt for ourselves or others.

****

For Men Only

Many women experience shame when they feel sexual in a situation that seems immoral or perverse. This is similar for men. But many men feel even more shame for not feeling sexual when they supposedly "should." When pornography is passed around or a dirty joke is told, they think a "real" man ought to enjoy and be aroused by the material. But what if you do not feel arousal, but actually feel disgust? The disgust calls into question your adequacy and potency as a man. In the same way, many men wait for a woman to initiate physical touch and sexual foreplay. They often do this because they fear rejection, but also because they feel sexual ambivalence: "What if I don't feel arousal when I should?"

8. Have you ever been in situations that caused you shame for not feeling sexual when a "real" man "should" feel arousal? Do you ever feel ashamed about feeling ambivalent about sexual situations or performance? If so, what conclusions do you tend to draw about your masculinity?

****

9. What aspects of ambivalence cause you shame? What do you not want others to know about you? Look back at the items you noted in questions 1 through 6.

Confused shame and contempt lead to a dizzying confusion of consequences inside us.

"I have desperately needed to talk regularly to T this past month. At the same time, I've been afraid of him, so afraid of his disapproval."

Intimacy=Sex=Danger

First the mixed horror/pleasure of abuse makes us extremely confused about intimacy. In our heads, intimacy (which we long for) is forever fused to sexuality (which we both desire and detest). Therefore, we reason, the longing for intimacy is a longing for sexual passion. But passion, as we have experienced it in abuse, destroys. Therefore, the longing for intimacy is dangerous and must be either avoided or conquered.

This equation of intimacy=sex=danger is called "sexualization of intimate relationships." It can make us think we're sexually attracted every time we start to care for someone of the opposite (and/or same) sex. Then, since sex=danger, we may either flee from the relationship or handle it as we handled our abuse.

We may confuse intimacy with sex at a variety of levels. For instance, we might not fantasize about having sex with a therapist, but merely about developing a friendship in which we are more special to the therapist than other clients. Intimacy is tinged with the idea of exclusivity and uniqueness appropriate to intercourse in marriage. Then, if intimate=exclusive=married, there is always a part of us that hopes any relationship will go deeper.

Therefore, because even the low-level intimacy of friendship is tinted with sex (which is dangerous) and pushes to go further, all involvement with others feels dangerous.

10. Can you identify with anything in this idea that intimacy=sex=danger? If you can, how does it look in your life?

_____ I can't make friends with members of the opposite (and/or same) sex. It usually feels like sexual attraction.

_____ I fantasize about being an exclusive or special friend to . . .

_____ Because intimacy is dangerous, I sabotage intimate relationships.

_____ I see myself as sexually dangerous to others, and I prove that by being a sexual predator.

_____ I see myself as sexually dangerous to others, so I protect them from me by . . .

_____ Other (name it):

It's important to realize that we can sexualize a relationship with either gender. A woman may hug another woman and feel that thrill of terror/pleasure that for her means this is intimacy; *therefore,* this is sexual; *therefore,* I want this to go deeper to exclusivity; *therefore,* this is dangerous.

The pleasure of intimacy produces a passion not just for more relationship, but for relationship on a deeper level.

The relationship may in fact go no further than casual talks and friendly hugs, while in one person's mind the longing for more either whispers or shouts in fantasies. It may deepen to the exclusivity of best friends. Or the "chemistry" (that is really confusion between intimacy and sex) may draw the two into a lesbian affair. This is not a sign that one or both was born "gay" and didn't know it. It is just the same kind of sexualization that occurs between a woman and a man.

But the agony of same-sex encounters is that the shame is far harsher. This woman, even if she just has fantasies, is guilty not only of lust but of perversion. Being attracted to a man is at least "normal."

It will be extremely hard for the man or woman who suffers with half-hated, half-enjoyed homosexual fantasies to cut past the rhetoric of the gay-bashing faction (which pushes the struggler into self-contempt) and the pro-gay movement (which urges contempt for gay-bashers). But until the person can lay aside shame and contempt long enough to let God's Spirit untangle the confusion, his or her efforts to stop the perverse thoughts will be frustrated.

11. Do you struggle with this same-sex confusion? Which of these sound like you?

_____ I have felt that "chemistry" with a member of the same gender.

_____ I have felt sexually attracted to someone of the same gender.

_____ I fantasize about an exclusive friendship with someone of my gender.

_____ I fantasize about sexual involvement with someone of my gender.

_____ I have a same-sex, exclusive friendship that is really precious to me. We're as close as married people, although we've never been sexually involved.

_____ I have had (or have now) a homosexual relationship.

12. This intimacy=sex confusion is (not surprisingly) confusing to talk about. If you had to explain to someone what you think goes on inside you when you sexualize relationships, what would you say?

> "My hatred for my longings for love have been greatest in relation to other men. My best friend in college provided a good example. He had a heart that was for my good and provided me with a taste of being loved, wanted, and enjoyed. Over time I became confused about the intensity of my love for my friend and at times even experienced sexual arousal. This became very confusing for me (I viewed myself as immoral), and I hated my longings for love and involvement. Even now I sometimes fear the possibility of sexualizing my longings in relationships and often envy those who were not abused and do not struggle with this problem."

Sex Replaces Intimacy

The other side of the confusion coin is that we may opt for sex rather than real intimacy. Perhaps sex feels more satisfying, because it gives us both the sense of fullness that comes from orgasm and the contemptuous revenge of violating the other person or ourselves. (More on relief and fullness and revenge in chapter 9.)

Sex may actually feel safer than intimacy. Intimacy requires that we have something inside to give, that we are willing to give it, and that we're willing to be affected by the other person. But we may feel we have nothing to offer except our bodies. Or, we may not want to be vulnerable to the other person. Or, we may have something inside to offer, but we may not be willing to give it because we don't want to affect the other person. There's something essentially wrong with us, we believe—didn't we partly want the abuse? So we're dangerous. We shouldn't be allowed access to another's soul.

We may react to this belief that sex is safer than intimacy by becoming promiscuous. Or, we may protect the world from our dangerous sexuality by being prim and proper but also obsessed with graphic sexual fantasies. Either the fantasies or the promiscuity has the bonus of confirming what we always feared: "I was right, I really am a whore."

13. Which, if any, of the following describes you?

_____ Sex meets my needs. I don't feel the need for some kind of emotional intimacy.

_____ Sex feels safer than intimacy because . . .

_____ I don't have anything someone of the opposite sex would want except my body.

_____ I'm dangerous to men/women because . . .

_____ I feel vile, dirty, cheap, or like a whore because . . .

_____ I'm promiscuous, and the way I feel about it is . . .

_____ I have graphic sexual fantasies, and the way I feel about that is . . .

As a bridegroom rejoices over his bride,
  so will your God rejoice over you. (Isaiah 62:5)

14. One of the most difficult concepts to embrace is God's extravagant gift of restoring our beauty. It is incredible to think that He rejoices passionately over us as a bridegroom. He actually enjoys the radiance of His bride.

a. What do you feel when you think of yourself as a stunningly beautiful bride?

b. What happens inside you when you think of God enjoying you as a bridegroom would?

c. Why do you suppose it's so hard for many of us to see ourselves as lovely? Why is the image of the dirty whore so difficult to give up?

"The image of being vile explains not only why the abuser betrayed the victim in the first place, but also gives reason for the absence of deep relationship today" (*The Wounded Heart*, page 155).

Gender=Sex=Perverse and Dangerous

Ambivalence also intertwines femaleness or maleness with shameful and perverse sexuality. Most abused women do not richly enjoy being women. Most abused men do not richly enjoy being men.

15. What signs can you see in your life that you don't deeply enjoy being a man or being a woman?

> *I despise women who have their hair done and their makeup perfect and*
> *their clothes feminine. I prefer pants and a wash-and-go haircut.*
> *I'd rather eat glass than flirt.*
> *I constantly have to prove to myself that I'm a man.*

Pleasure=Danger

If any level of pleasure in relationship is dangerous, and sexual pleasure is dangerous, then pretty soon any inner or physical pleasure is dangerous. A certain degree of pleasure (in a good meal, good sex, good party with friends) may seem okay, but for many of us, pleasure beyond the danger zone is off limits. We have to watch and control both longings and pleasures to make sure they don't get out of hand. If a relationship or success begins to give us joy, we have to crack down to make sure we don't go wild.

16. Do you place limits on your pleasure? If so, in what areas do you draw lines?

> "How does one describe the kind of ambivalence I've been experiencing this past week? It's like cold, abrasive chains around my heart that rub raw the flesh with every breath I take. Such unbelievable anxiety over the possibility of making the wrong decision."

_____ Enjoying someone of the opposite sex too much.

_____ Enjoying a same-sex friend too much.

_____ Enjoying a physical activity, such as a sport, too much.

_____ Enjoying music too much.

_____ Enjoying success at work too much.

_____ Other (name it):

Longing and Passion=Danger

17. Check the sentences that apply to you.

_____ Any kind of deep passion in me terrifies me.

_____ I try to numb the mixed desire-for/hatred-of sexual passion by . . .

     _____ having sex a lot.

     _____ fantasizing about sex.

     _____ masturbating.

_____ I feel no sexual desire.

_____ I turn my mind off during sex.

_____ If a sexual thought enters my brain, I pounce on it and destroy it.

_____ I've chosen a partner who doesn't stir my passions because he (she) . . .

     _____ thinks sex=love.

     _____ has to have sex all the time.

     _____ is uncomfortable with his (her) manhood (womanhood).

     _____ is abusive.

> "I want intimacy, but I am afraid of it. 'Come in and I will be your friend, but if you get too close, I can shut down.'"

     _____ is distant.

Other (name it):

18. Nonsexual longings can also be associated with that cheap, dangerous pleasure. Which of these sounds like you?

____ When I want to be noticed, I feel alternately lustful and dangerous, and then cheap and frightened.

____ I back away from compliments so that I won't start longing for warmth and appreciation.

____ When someone is warm to me, I first feel like clinging to them for dear life. Then I feel ashamed of that feeling and back away.

____ I have to protect people from my emotions and/or sexuality.

19. Is there anything else you do because you view your longings as dangerous? Explain.

Addictions and Compulsions

All compulsions—from perfectionism to eating disorders to sexual addictions and perversion—have a hold on us because they achieve two things we deeply desire: *relief* and *revenge*. Relief is easier to comprehend. A chronic masturbator or overeater obviously experiences pleasure from the orgasm or dessert. However, such pleasure does not explain why an exhibitionist would risk his reputation and career for an orgasm he could obtain in many safer ways. The addiction provides revenge as well as relief.

"Revenge is the working out of deep-soul hatred toward others (other-centered contempt) or toward oneself (self-contempt). Revenge exacts payment against both the perpetrator of the past harm and the victim for her supposed cooperation and ambivalent pleasure. At times the symptom pattern is more obviously connected to self-contempt (masochism, being the object of battering or anal sex) and at other times toward other-centered contempt (sadism, predatory sexual promiscuity, seductive Don Juanism). More often, however, both sides of revenge (contempt) are played out in the same behavior. . . . The compulsive cycle looks something like this: longing, disappointment, power (other-centered revenge), shame (self-contempt), self-hatred, penance.

"Sexual dysfunction or compulsiveness [as well as other compulsions] is often a sign of undealt-with rage. The rage that is worked out through self-and other-centered contempt must be exposed and connected to the past abuse if it is to lose its compulsive edge. The dilemma is that shame masks not only the symptom but also the role of revenge" (*The Wounded Heart*, pages 164-165).

20. It's not always easy to see how a compulsion achieves revenge. But think about your compulsions. How do they each provide relief and revenge for you?

COMPULSION	PROVIDES RELIEF BY	PROVIDES REVENGE BY
Fantasy/ masturbation	*Orgasm without risk of rejection or loss of control.*	*Others: power over someone's passion.* *Self: shame proves I'm a whore.*
Anorexia	*Makes me feel in control of at least something.*	*Others: no one can keep me from killing myself.* *Self: I'll destroy my hated body.*

21. Compulsions and sexual dysfunction give us a chance to take revenge against someone and so express hidden rage. Against whom or what do you suppose you might be furious? Why do you think you desire revenge against someone?

22. Why do you suppose you find such relief through the means you have? What is it about this kind of relief that is so important to you?

23. Look back over your responses to questions 1 through 22—the roots of your ambivalence and the damage it has caused you. Then set a timer for twenty minutes. Take that time to write what goes through your mind when you think of these things. You can use this page and the next, or write in your own journal.

Write down the feelings you have, the way your body reacts, the events or effects that most hurt or anger you, the things you really want to change and why you find it hard—whatever's in your mind. You can spend the whole time writing about one current situation that raises issues of ambivalence, or you can write about something specific in the past.

> "I left with wings on my feet and a song in my heart. (It's phrases like that that bring the greatest self-contempt. I choke on the words as I write them.)"

Continue journal writing on this page.

24. Go back and circle or underline statements in your journal writing that seem especially significant.

For Group Discussion

The sexualization of intimacy is a tough concept to grasp. You may need to discuss the idea before you talk about specific examples. Why do abuse victims confuse sex with intimacy? Why do we view intimacy, gender, sex, and pleasure as dangerous?

Question 23, the mindstream exercise, would be a good one to focus on. It can also be a subject of prayer as you end. What would you like God to do about the damage you've suffered?

---

25. How would you summarize the way ambivalence makes you treat yourself, others, and God?

MYSELF

> "I doubt myself when I am ambivalent, thus I don't make decisions, I don't make commitments, I won't express my feelings because I always have two or three and I'm not sure which is the right one or the most dominant."

OTHERS

GOD

26. Consider portraying your feelings of ambivalence in a collage or with crayons.

Does God Understand Ambivalence?

Has God ever experienced ambivalence? Not really. James asserts that God "does not change like shifting shadows" (James 1:17). Instead of feeling ambivalent, God seems to be perfectly content with opposites and paradoxes. "I live in a high and holy place," He says, "but also with him who is contrite and lowly in spirit" (Isaiah 57:15). God is a Lion and a Lamb, relentless and tender, wrathful and compassionate, just and forgiving. And He isn't pulled apart or tossed helplessly between poles. He is able to hate sin and love people, or to be Three and One at the same time, with perfect peace and consistency.

While on earth, Jesus willingly chose to experience powerlessness (even though all power was at His disposal) and betrayal (even though He could have defended Himself). Jesus also chose to face ambivalence. First He chose to be both God and man, and to endure less-than-divine messages from His mortal body: I'm hungry, I'm tired, I feel pain. Just before He launched the public phase of His mission, He spent forty days alone and fasting to totally commit His whole self to the task. The devil tried to shake Jesus' resolve, but He hung on. (See Luke 4:1-13.)

Then, just before His arrest, Jesus felt blood-sweating ambivalence (Luke 22:44).

As committed as He was to His mission, Jesus refused to deny that He strongly desired not to be tortured and die. Wanting two things at once—both to be obedient to His Father and to retain the intimacy He had always known with the Father and the Spirit—caused Him intense anguish. He had never been separated from the Father and Spirit, but now He was about to become for a time the sin they detested. And of course, as a man He was going to face horrible physical pain.

"My soul is overwhelmed with sorrow to the point of death," He told His closest friends, asking them to stay awake and watch for His betrayer's arrival while He wrestled with His inner conflict (Mark 14:34). He resolved His struggle enough to see His mission through without flinching, even though the agony of separation was intense. And having chosen to be human, He couldn't do anything about His body's loud protests against beatings and crucifixion. Bodies (as abuse victims know well) respond as they were built to respond, no matter what contrary decisions their owners make.

27. Think about Jesus' experience of ambivalence. You can read Mark 14:32-42. Then write a letter to Jesus telling Him how it makes you feel to think that He chose to suffer the anguish of conflicting desires. If it all seems unreal to you—just words—tell Him so. You can also tell Him about your own struggles with ambivalence, and you can ask Him for help.

Since the children have flesh and blood, he too shared in their humanity so that by his death he might destroy him who holds the power of death—that is, the devil—and free those who all their lives were held in slavery by their fear of death. . . . Because he himself suffered when he was tempted, he is able to help those who are being tempted. (Hebrews 2:14-15,18)

For Group Discussion

Read aloud to the group as much of your letters to Jesus as you feel comfortable sharing. As you hear each letter, offer feedback. How do you feel hearing that letter? What do you appreciate about it? What did you learn about the reader or yourself?

CHAPTER NINE

BETRAYAL

The Deed

If an enemy were insulting me,
I could endure it;
if a foe were raising himself against me,
I could hide from him.
But it is you, a man like myself,
my companion, my close friend,
with whom I once enjoyed sweet fellowship
as we walked with the throng at the house of God. (Psalm 55:12-14)

It is shattering to be betrayed by someone to whom we have entrusted something of our heart: a neighbor, a family friend, a teacher. And what words can describe a child betrayed by the members of her own family? Her parents have neglected their sacred responsibilities to nourish their child's soul and to protect it and her body from attack. Her abuser has offered her intimacy and then has shown the gift to be a lie. It may even seem that her body and soul have betrayed her by longing for and enjoying touch and closeness from an enemy.

Betrayal can be defined as *"any disregard or harm done to the dignity of another as a result of one's commitment to find life apart from God" (The Wounded Heart, page 129.)* This is so common in a sinful world—a merchant sells us an inferior product, a friend tells us a lie—that we often fail to notice it as betrayal.

We may prefer to tell ourselves that "it just happened" because it is so devastating to see ourselves as a victim of a carefully orchestrated plot. But as much as we may like to believe that our abuser merely stumbled in a moment of weakness, the fact is that he framed us through the stages we examined in chapter 4: alluring us with an offer of special intimacy; physical contact that appeared appropriate; sexual abuse proper; threats and/or privileges to silence us.

To prove a point about His Father's faithfulness, Jesus asked, "Which of you fathers, if your son asks for a fish, will give him a snake instead? Or if he asks for an egg, will give him a scorpion?" (Luke 11:11-12). The abused child in the crowd can only raise his hand and reply, "My father and mother gave me snakes and scorpions, or

> "I lived for years with a rigid commitment to never, *never* let anyone into my life again. If you make yourself vulnerable, you only open yourself up to pain, humiliation, rejection. I gave up the ridiculous notion that I could really live life; I'd better settle for just getting through it as best I could. Day by day, year by year, I erected a set of my very own 'deflector shields' that effectively insulated me from emotional interaction with my world. At least I wasn't in agony. In fact, I was so numb I didn't feel much of anything."

nothing at all. Why should I expect God to be any different?"

Read pages 127-141 of *The Wounded Heart*. You'll notice that the betrayal of abuse has three levels: (1) the family's failure to nourish the child prior to the abuse, (2) the treachery of the abuser, (3) and the lack of protection offered by the non-offending parent(s). If the family had provided the respect and compassion the child needed, she would not have been so thirsty as to drink the abuser's polluted water. Caring for a child is a parent's sacred duty; to fail in that, for whatever reason and to whatever degree, is betrayal. Likewise, the abuser's deceitful setup was an invitation to trust that proved false. Finally, the parents' failure to provide a safe place to run after the abuse allows the anger and shame to send down deep roots into the soil of secrecy.

Here is the betrayal of abuse: *"The victim of abuse is left thirsty and then is forced to participate in consuming something that both touches the legitimate thirst of her being, while also destroying the very aspect of her being that has been relationally aroused"* (*The Wounded Heart*, page 131).

1. How did your abuser betray his or her offer of intimacy?

2. How do you feel when you think about that now? What is your body doing? What do you feel like doing?

"I envisioned being blamed, punished and rejected [by my parents]. They would see me as flawed and bad as I viewed myself. Revelation of my heinous sins was certain to cut off the little love and protection that I experienced by being a good boy and not adding to the pain of my parents."

3. Do you recall feeling betrayed at the time? If you do, what was that like?

4. Look back over pages 131-133 of the book. How did your nonoffending parent(s) fail to nurture or protect you?

Parent 1, my (choose one) father/stepfather/mother/stepmother/other (specify)

_____ was an accomplice by . . .

_____ chose neglect or denial by . . .

_____ provided no place to turn after the abuse because . . .

Parent 2, my (choose one) father/stepfather/mother/stepmother/other (specify)

_____ was an accomplice by . . .

_____ chose neglect or denial by . . .

_____ provided no place to turn after the abuse because . . .

If you had more than two parents—for example, if you had two natural and two step-parents—write about the others' betrayal in your journal.

5. How are you feeling about your nonoffending parent(s)?

6. Facing exactly how we've been betrayed should help us feel and come to terms with our anger. (Anger is not the final stop on our journey, but it is one necessary stop.) Do you have trouble feeling angry at your parent(s) or your perpetrator? If so, why do you suppose that is?

7. If you do feel anger toward your parents, what have you done with that anger? (Have you taken it out as contempt toward yourself or toward your parents?)

What Has Betrayal Done in Me?
8. Check the statements that sound like you.

Hypervigilance
_____ I keep a sharp lookout for people who might stab me in the back.

_____ I'm extremely self-conscious about what other people may secretly think of me.

_____ I watch my every move to make sure I don't do anything I'll regret.

For Group Discussion

If you've tended to minimize or excuse what your family or abuser(s) have done, it may be hard for you to put their betrayal into words, especially aloud. However, doing this can help you get past that denial. If you really had trouble answering questions 1 through 6, the others in your group may be able to help you now that they've heard some of your story.

Suspiciousness of Others, Self, and God

____ I deflect compliments because I don't trust the source.

____ Compliments make me feel vulnerable, unsafe.

____ I'm afraid that if I let go and express my anger against someone, I could do serious damage.

____ I don't trust myself around members of the opposite sex.

____ I am very slow to trust people.

____ When I like a man/woman, I tend to assume it's sexual attraction.

____ I have trouble believing God is really trustworthy.

> "The feeling of abandonment is quite clear as an over-reaction and I can name it and deal with it now. A simple thing like my husband driving in a car ahead of me, and I was supposed to be following yet he went too fast and made a turn into traffic and lost me sent me into anger and abandonment. . . . In the past I used my husband's failures toward me to excuse pulling away from him. I now know that I have the capacity and responsibility to love a man who fails me."

Distortion and Denial About Relationships

____ I have trouble reading people's moods and feelings.

____ When I enter a room, I immediately "read the room," checking out who's there, what they're doing, what their mood is, and how they respond to my arrival.

____ I don't trust my intuitions about relationships.

____ When I was a child, people told me I was feeling something other than what I thought I was feeling.

____ Some people still tell me what I'm feeling.

____ My intuition about _____ makes me uncomfortable.

____ I excuse or have excused my abuser's behavior.

____ I excuse other people's wrong behavior. I tend not to hold them responsible or confront them.

____ I am protecting someone's reputation by concealing the truth about his or her behavior.

____ I have protected someone like this in the past.

Severe betrayal causes us to lose hope for intimacy, strength, and justice in relationship. We conclude that no relationship can be safely enjoyed, trusted, or expected to last.

9. Again, check the statements that sound like you.

Lost Hope for Intimacy

____ I'm not deeply intimate with anyone.

____ I don't like people to get too close.

> "I have had trouble trusting women with the deeper parts of my soul. They give me their hearts, but I seldom find one I give myself to. I test them with little parts. . . . Being in leadership makes me even more guarded. I have never put all my eggs in one basket. Many know parts of me. No one knows all."

____ I have many friends and associates, but no one really knows what goes on inside me.

____ My marriage works, but I wouldn't talk with my spouse about the deep longings and pains in my soul.

____ My spouse and I are open or secret enemies.

____ Every time I think I'm really getting close to someone, it seems as though the relationship falls apart.

____ I like to keep busy at work/play. When I'm alone doing nothing in particular, I don't like how I feel.

____ I don't think of God as someone I can be close to.

Lost Hope for Strength and Justice

____ I don't like feeling vulnerable.

____ I would rather protect myself than have to depend on someone else.

____ I believe in the saying, "The Lord helps those who help themselves."

> "I lost my ability to perceive who was safe and who was not. [Therefore,] I did not set good boundaries."

____ I have asked/am still asking myself, "How could I have been so stupid as to trust someone so untrustworthy?" I never want to do that again.

____ I think God is frequently unjust.

Finally, a victim of betrayal tends to think something deeply wrong with her must have caused the betrayal. Instead of saying, "My mother failed to value me as I deserved to be valued," she says, "I must not have be worth much if my mother treated me that way."

10. Again, check the statements that sound true of you, and complete the sentences.

____ I feel ugly because . . .

____ I feel undesirable because . . .

____ I pay a lot of attention to my physique.

____ I make sure I exercise every day.

____ I'm nearly always on a diet.

____ I don't pay much attention to what I eat.

____ I weigh myself at least once a day.

____ I don't do much to make myself look feminine/masculine.

____ I spend a lot of time each day making myself look beautiful/handsome/trendy.

____ How I look is very important to me.

____ I feel bad that I'm not good at making friends.

____ I'm not the kind of person people enjoy at parties.

____ I like to learn skills and build my self-confidence so that I'll be better at relationships.

____ I'm painfully shy.

11. Does it seem to help you at all to know that the traits and habits you checked are connected to the betrayal of your abuse? Why, or why not?

> "What I am most aware of is how I am suspicious that others genuinely desire my well-being, and even if they do I am distrustful that they will be able to help. I learned that the only one I can trust is myself."

12. Take a minute or two to read over the experiences and effects of betrayal that you've noted in this chapter. Then set a timer for twenty minutes. During that time, focus on one person who has betrayed you. It might be your childhood abuser, a parent, or someone else in your life right now. Take twenty minutes without stopping to write what goes through your mind when you think of what that person has done/is doing to you. Use the space below and on the next page, or you can write in your own journal.

Write down the feelings you have, the way your body reacts, the events or effects that most hurt or anger you, the excuses you can think of to let the person off the hook, the reasons why those excuses are or aren't convincing—in short, whatever comes to mind. Remember that grammar and spelling don't count; your only requirement is to keep writing until the timer sounds.

Continue journal writing on this page.

If you find it profitable, go back and circle or underline statements in this journal writing that you find especially significant.

13. Look back at the items you checked in this section, and try to summarize how betrayal affects the way you view and treat yourself, others, and God.

YOURSELF

OTHERS

GOD

For Group Discussion

Question 13 is the key one for discussion. Pull in specifics from earlier questions as you like.

How do you feel when you talk about how betrayal has damaged you? Take some time to tell God your feelings and ask Him to overcome these effects in you.

---

14. When you think about your betrayal, what picture comes to mind? Describe it or draw it.

Does God Understand Betrayal?

God had never experienced powerlessness until He took on human flesh, but betrayal He has known since before humans existed. When the first humans lived in Eden, already there was a serpent who, even though he was one of God's creatures, was his Creator's sworn enemy. But the man and woman were God's masterpiece, for they possessed certain of God's qualities that none of His other creatures had. They possessed not only His ability to make moral choices and His delight in inventing things that had not existed before. They also possessed His passion, His ability to love. He intended them to be not just servants, but family.

Surely no one has ever owed anyone absolute loyalty more than Adam and Eve owed God. He had given them life and each other. He had entrusted to them the rule of an entire planet. He had offered them His love. But they rejected Him.

God's response was not furious rage, but sorrow and a loving commitment to do whatever it would take to restore them. When it was clear that they had twisted their souls beyond simple mending, He altered their bodies and their world in ways that would allow eventual healing. Then He embarked on an intricate plan to win back His beloved species.

A few humans have received glimpses of God's heart. He asked one man to marry an unfaithful woman, allow her to become a prostitute and a slave, then buy her back (Hosea 1:2–3:7). In this way, Hosea tasted the betrayal God felt as a jilted lover.

"I long to redeem them
but they speak lies against me.
They do not cry out to me from their hearts
but wail upon their beds. . . .
I trained them and strengthened them,
but they plot evil against me. . . .

"How can I give you up, Ephraim?
How can I hand you over, Israel? . . .
My heart is changed within me;
all my compassion is aroused.
I will not carry out my fierce anger,
nor will I turn and devastate Ephraim.
For I am God, and not man—
the Holy One among you.
I will not come in wrath."
(Hosea 7:13-15, 11:8-9)

"A few weeks ago I had thought about the fact that we'd be leaving and there would have to be a 'goodbye' sometime—and what's a farewell without a good hug! As soon as I thought that, I had one of these flashes of violence—seeing myself giving T a hug and simultaneously being slashed back and forth viciously from head to foot down my back with a machete. I was actually killed. It was the most violent of these mental flashes that I've ever had. Who does this? Is it me? Why this fear? Maybe because T has been the most dangerous person in my life lately. One, he knows me. Two, I need him. What more potentially dangerous situation can there be for me!?"

"I will not come in wrath." Instead, He came as a man healing, forgiving, embracing. A band of men and women swore loyalty to Jesus; twelve of them were His intimate friends.

Then one of the Twelve—the one called Judas Iscariot—went to the chief priests and asked, "What are you willing to give me if I hand him over to you?" So they counted out for him thirty silver coins. From then on Judas watched for an opportunity to hand him over. . . .
When evening came, Jesus was reclining at the table with the Twelve. And while they were eating, he said, "I tell you the truth, one of you will betray me."
They were very sad and began to say to him one after the other, "Surely not I, Lord?" . . .
Then Judas, the one who would betray him, said, "Surely not I, Rabbi?" Jesus answered, "Yes, it is you." . . .
Then Jesus told them, "This very night you will all fall away on account of me. . . ."
Peter replied, "Even if all fall away on account of you, I never will."
"I tell you the truth," Jesus answered, "this very night, before the rooster crows, you will disown me three times." . . .
Then Jesus went with his disciples to a place called Gethsemane. (Matthew 26:14-16,20-22,25,31-34,36)

Judas, one of the Twelve, arrived. With him was a large crowd armed with swords and clubs, sent from the chief priests and the elders of the people. Now the betrayer had arranged a signal with them: "The one I kiss is the man; arrest him." Going at once to Jesus, Judas said, "Greetings, Rabbi!" and kissed him.
Jesus replied, "Friend, do what you came for."
Then the men stepped forward, seized Jesus and arrested him. . . .
Then all the disciples deserted him and fled. (Matthew 26:47-50,56)

Peter did disown Jesus three times that night to protect himself. The crowds who had hailed Jesus as King less than a week before turned on Him when it became clear that He was not the military leader they had hoped for. He was sentenced to death. Only a few of His female disciples dared show up at His execution; the men feared arrest.

Jesus' official crime was recorded as treason. But in fact, His executioners were doing only what His people had been doing since Adam: trying to erase God from existence so they could run their own lives. He took their treason into Himself, allowed it to kill Him, then offered them forgiveness.

15. What difference (if any) does it make to you that God understands your betrayal from experience?

16. How are you feeling right now? What do you feel like doing?

17. Is there anything you'd like to say to God right now? Write it down.

STYLE OF RELATING

Offering or Protecting?

Probably all abuse victims suffer the effects of powerlessness, ambivalence, and betrayal to some degree. Many of us express that damage outwardly through a fairly predictable set of secondary symptoms: depression, sexual dysfunction or addiction, compulsions, physical ailments, low self-esteem. (Review your responses in chapter 2 of this guide.) However, different attitudes may lie behind the same symptom in two people. And some people seem to exhibit none of these typical symptoms of abuse.

For both of these reasons, if you want to discern the precise damage and unloving attitudes that control your unique soul, you will usually have more success if you look at secondary symptoms in a wider context: your *style of relating*.

Pages 168-185 of *The Wounded Heart* discuss styles of relating in detail. A relational style is defined there as *the characteristic manner of both offering and protecting oneself in social interactions*. Your style of relating is a window to your heart:

> *"Each tree is recognized by its own fruit. People do not pick figs from thornbushes, or grapes from briers. The good man brings good things out of the good stored up in his heart, and the evil man brings evil things out of the evil stored up in his heart. For out of the overflow of his heart his mouth speaks." (Luke 6:44-45)*

The way we treat God and other people—in other words, how we relate—is a clue to how we really feel about God. (See Mark 12:28-34.) Do we love selflessly, passionately, boldly? Or are we committed to self-protection, to the vow that we will not be hurt again? Love and self-protection are opposites; we can't do the first if we are committed to the second. Why not? Because love pursues what is best for the other person even at a high cost to oneself, whereas self-protection pursues what seems best for oneself even at a high cost to the other person. At the very least, self-protection hinders us from doing good, and it often motivates us to use and overlook people in hurtful ways, as our abusers have done to us.

The reason we develop self-protective styles is very reasonable: People have repeatedly abused us when we could not protect ourselves, and no one else protected us. As people made in God's image we naturally hate to feel alone, unloved, and used. So, we reason, "If no one else is looking out for me, I will never survive unless I look out for myself." The core assumption is that God is not looking out for us. And if "looking out for us" means keeping us from hurting, He is certainly not doing that. He has another agenda entirely: not making us pain free, but freeing us to know what it means to love and be loved.

Always

Organize your life

ability to
handle the job ┌Mother

PROFESSIONAL
INITIATIVE

Set priorities **maintain**

authority **confidence**

face crisis control

definite **Tireless** 'loyalty'
correct effort
smartest

Plan carefully

"I can make a contribution

lay groundwork

manager

Women

preparing

supervisor

taking

think

Best director

the lead

impressive

ORGANIZE

measures up

OPINION best ideas

Expectations

decides **advances** fighting

career A higher standard of living

Distinction

Independence **SUCCESS**

WORKS

Logic

in the driver's seat

good experience

Law-and-order direction

right observation

wise decisions

accomplished

perfection dominate

Responsibility

force

Polite

rule

learning

perform

Improving

produce

powerful

plan **push**

ABSOLUTE OUR WAY

NO HASSLE

BUSINESS
economic

savings CASH

Working mother

budget

Correct your spelling

How Do I Relate?

Pages 174-185 of *The Wounded Heart* outline three broad patterns that are common for women who have been sexually abused. (Women who have not been sexually abused may also exhibit these patterns. As with checklists in previous chapters, these should not be construed as proof that one has been abused.) A man can learn a great deal about women and even himself by looking over this section.

After reading the section in *The Wounded Heart*, use the checklists that follow to identify features of your relational style. (Notice that some of the features are not necessarily bad in themselves. In later questions you'll have a chance to evaluate the attitudes behind your habits.) Checklists for men begin on page 146 of this guide.

The Good Girl

_____ I place a high priority on helping other people.

_____ One of my main goals is to keep peace and avoid conflict with others.

_____ I feel a lot of contempt for myself, but I try not to let others know about it.

_____ I secretly struggle with sexual fantasies.

_____ I feel enormous guilt about my fantasies, but I can't stop.

_____ I have little or no interest in sex.

_____ My mind tends to go elsewhere during sex.

_____ I have trouble standing up to aggressive people or evildoers.

_____ I feel guilty if I'm angry at someone.

_____ If I feel hurt, I tell myself I'm overreacting or push myself to forgive. It feels selfish to dwell on hurt.

_____ I rarely lose my temper.

_____ I am an energetic worker.

_____ I'm more passive than assertive or aggressive.

_____ I think people find me pleasant.

_____ I feel lonely.

_____ I like to be in control, especially of myself.

_____ I don't like to impose on other people.

_____ I like my environment to be organized, but I rarely feel I have the chaos in order.

_____ I have trouble protecting my spouse or children from harm.

> "After a lifetime of hurts, I gave up on trusting anyone or wanting anything from relationships. Therefore, I became very caught up in performance—I would have the cleanest house in the world. My kids would be the model kids. I would work tirelessly for the church and the school. The best piano teacher, the best mother, the best wife, the best *everything*. My motto was, 'I will make my world perfect,' and the next part of the sentence was, 'and don't you dare cross me.' But perfectionism created a wall that got thicker as I got lonelier and soon no one was there to see my accomplishments because I had walled them all out. By being alone in my world, I felt safe from the exposure of another."

_____ I'm not good at delegating tasks to others (especially adults).

_____ I tend to turn compliments aside with comments like "It was nothing," by giving the Lord the credit, or by pointing out the flaws in what I've done.

_____ Before I started dealing with my abuse, I recalled some events, but I didn't see it as all that important, or I blamed myself.

_____ I tend to be busy up to, and often beyond, my real capacity.

> "Since I could never rely upon those closest to provide emotional support, I learned to do it myself. I became very competent and disciplined and learned to cover my bases in case the unexpected occurred. My self-contempt also motivated me to try hard to meet the expectations of others so that I would not be found lacking or inadequate."

_____ I'd rather do something good for someone than give him or her a glimpse of my soul.

_____ I have trouble saying no.

_____ I avoid asking for help.

_____ I apologize a lot more than I receive apologies.

_____ I am critical of myself, especially as a woman.

_____ As I child I was a great helper, even perhaps to my abuser.

_____ As a child I was a good listener and generally quiet—not a troublemaker.

The Tough Girl

_____ I see myself as a take-charge, task-oriented person.

_____ I have tended to view my longings as sentimental, sloppy, and/or weak.

_____ I hate to be dependent on people.

_____ When I feel sexual, I feel more powerful than desirable.

_____ I sometimes fantasize about dominating men.

_____ When people compliment me, I wonder what they're after.

_____ I can usually tell when people are being dishonest or untrustworthy.

_____ I am highly competent at a variety of tasks.

_____ I like to be in charge.

> "'Being a needy little girl is ugly. Vulnerability is repulsive. One ought to keep her neediness private, as she would a heinous sin. Weakness is despicable, demeaning, death.' That couldn't express better how I feel."

_____ When challenged, I am willing to go toe to toe with anyone to accomplish what I think is right.

_____ I lose my temper fairly frequently.

_____ I don't put much stock in compliments.

_____ People value me for my competence.

_____ I have strong opinions about women's rights.

_____ Nobody would dare call me cuddly or soft.

_____ When I feel threatened or angry, I tend to be verbally aggressive or sarcastic to overpower the other person.

_____ I can be wonderfully pleasant, but people know they'll be sorry if they cross my line.

The Party Girl

_____ I really like a good time.

_____ I'm hard to pin down.

_____ You can count on my being unpredictable.

_____ I have moderate or wild mood swings.

_____ I'm easily hurt.

_____ I tend to feel it's pointless to dwell on hurts.

> "I operated under the assumption that if I gave you a reason to shun me or hate me it was better than longing for involvement and not getting it. I enmeshed people by taking of them and trying to be all they wanted, all the time hating them for never giving me what I wanted."

_____ I try not to let things bother me, but often they do.

_____ I take things out of context or mishear them.

_____ I am whiny sometimes and bold at other times.

_____ I often feel very afraid, but at other times I'm surprisingly brave.

_____ I'm fickle.

_____ I'm not good at keeping long-term relationships.

_____ When a relationship starts to get too close, I want to end it so I . . .

 _____ pull away.

 _____ cause conflict.

 _____ do something disloyal.

 _____ get attracted to another man.

 _____ Other (name it):

_____ I get out of a relationship when the person demands too much time and energy.

_____ I feel uncomfortable with commitment.

_____ I receive many advances from the opposite sex; and I'm surprised, wondering why the person is attracted.

_____ I flirt a lot.

_____ I enjoy being seductive.

2. Photocopy the checklist on pages 143-144, and ask someone who knows you well to fill it out. For a broader survey, ask several people who know you in different contexts. Ask the person to be as honest as possible and not to take responsibility for shielding you from the truth. (Limited permission is given to copy these worksheets for use in conjunction with your study of *The Wounded Heart*. No pages in any other part of this book may be copied, nor may the worksheets be copied for any reason other than actual use with this book.)

Please don't give anyone this checklist unless you really feel prepared to hear some painful truth. We'll feel terrible if you use the information you gain to load yourself with guilt for being so unlovable, or to confirm your suspicion that this person really despises you, or as an excuse to stage an emotional scene designed to get attention. And your friend will probably be frustrated if you ask him or her to tell you the truth and then get angry when he or she does what you asked.

Items 1 through 18 are traits of a Good Girl. Items 19 through 38 describe a Tough Girl. Items 39 through 57 indicate a Party Girl.

3. Look over the results of your checklist and your friend(s) checklist(s). Which of these does it look as though you are primarily?

_____ Good Girl

_____ Tough Girl

_____ Party Girl

_____ None of these

4. Perhaps you don't seem to fall perfectly into one category. Perhaps you think none of these categories describes you. What else do you notice about your style of relating?

> *I tend to be a Good Girl at home and a Tough Girl at work.*
> *I'd really like to think of myself as a Good Girl, and I really do feel guilty if I upset someone or get angry. But at the core I'm a Party Girl. I play the martyr to get sympathy, but if the relationship gets costly, I get out.*

How Do Others Experience Me?

Your friend has asked you to fill out this checklist, marking the items that you believe are true of her fairly often. She probably doesn't *always* act as a given item describes, only on a regular basis. In giving you this checklist, your friend is taking a risk, putting some trust in you. We hope you'll respect that trust by telling her what you really think, confronting her if she tries to punish you for being honest, and not telling anyone else about the checklist or what you've observed about your friend.

My friend . . .

1. ____ loves to help people and do favors.

2. ____ places a high value on keeping the peace.

3. ____ is pleasant, but rarely passionate.

4. ____ rarely loses her temper.

5. ____ rarely invites me to know what's going on inside her.

6. ____ is an energetic worker and organizer.

7. ____ avoids asking for help.

8. ____ hates to impose on people.

9. ____ is very concerned with what people think of her.

10. ____ rarely laughs uncontrollably.

11. ____ plays the martyr.

12. ____ gets depressed when someone tells her she's withholding herself, or when confronted on another issue.

13. ____ can't stand to say no.

14. ____ hates conflict or having people upset with her.

15. ____ apologizes a lot.

16. ____ insists that people be pleased with her.

17. ____ invites people to take her for granted.

18. ____ is quietly, pleasantly detached from deep involvement with people.

19. ____ rarely expresses soft feelings, such as tenderness, sorrow, or fear.

20. ____ tends to be take-charge, task-oriented, and no-nonsense.

21. ____ avoids appearing weak.

22. ____ is easy to respect.

23. ____ is easy to fear.

24. ____ loses her temper often.

25. ____ is sensitive when snubbed.

26. ____ is suspicious of others' motives.

27. ____ tends to be critical.

28. ____ likes to air her own opinions.

29. ____ is impressively competent at practically everything she tries.

30. ____ acts like a know-it-all.

My friend . . .

31. ____ likes to have the last word.

32. ____ doesn't let people get close to her.

33. ____ can silence people with a look.

34. ____ has a biting wit.

35. ____ seems too busy to focus on a person.

36. ____ expects to be in charge.

37. ____ will go toe to toe with people who cross or compete with her.

38. ____ is not a person most people enjoy for herself, but rather for her abilities.

39. ____ is hard to pin down.

40. ____ has wild or moderate, but noticeable mood swings.

41. ____ is inconsistent and fickle.

42. ____ can be warm one minute and demanding or whining the next.

43. ____ can be whiny one day and surprisingly brave the next.

44. ____ is easily hurt.

45. ____ takes things out of context or mishears them.

46. ____ uses sexuality to seduce people into doing what she wants.

47. ____ uses fragile health or emotions to manipulate people into giving her her way.

48. ____ flirts a lot.

49. ____ receives advances from men and acts surprised.

50. ____ goes into depression when someone wounds her.

51. ____ tries to keep her spouse or children dependent on her.

52. ____ loves in a demanding way.

53. ____ makes a person feel deeply needed.

54. ____ makes me feel guilty when I let her down.

55. ____ gets out of relationships when they cost too much.

56. ____ makes me feel I could never do enough to make her happy.

57. ____ is confusing and frustrating.

5. Consider these attitudes that often lie behind each style. Which of these do you suspect might be behind your relational style? Some sentences need completing.

The Good Girl

____ I feel contempt for myself because of . . .

____ Being uninterested in sex is a great way to take revenge on . . .

____ Guilt controls me.

____ I lack the courage and humility to impose on others. I refuse to risk being rejected.

____ I'm terrified of anger and rejection. Protecting myself from those is a top priority.

____ I'm unwilling to take the risk involved in revealing my soul to people.

____ My apologies are self-centered; they are demands that other people reaffirm that I'm wanted.

____ I'm secretly angry at a lot of people; but it's unsafe to express that anger openly. Instead, I simply withhold my heart from them.

____ I don't necessarily have to be in control of others, but I have to be in control of myself.

The Tough Girl

____ I believe I'm above most kinds of emotions.

____ I'm suspicious of others' motives.

____ I'm arrogant. I think I'm smarter, more efficient, more skilled, or better in some other way than most of the people I deal with.

____ I view other people with a great deal of contempt.

____ I think neediness is childish.

____ I refuse to be dependent on anyone.

____ Emotions got me into trouble in the first place. I refuse to let feelings cause me pain anymore.

____ I am extremely angry.

____ I want to be in control, not just of myself, but of other people.

_____ I don't trust people to get too close.

_____ I think people's gestures of kindness are really ploys to get me to trust them so they can take advantage of me.

_____ I intimidate people so they'll keep their distance.

_____ I refuse to be found wrong.

The Party Girl

_____ I view everyone with contempt—myself as well as others.

_____ I'm strongly ambivalent; it's hard for me to decide who I hate more, myself or others.

_____ I'm extremely afraid.

_____ It's hard for me to decide whether I hunger for relationships more than I fear them.

_____ I feel no guilt about using people and then throwing them away.

_____ I like to seduce people with either lust or guilt into doing what I want.

_____ I'm always dissatisfied.

****

For Men Only

Men also build styles of relating from the mortar of contempt. The self-contemptuous man tends to be a Nice Boy who avoids conflict and decisions. The other-centered contemptuous man, or what we will call the Macho Boy, uses anger, intimidation, and power to subjugate others to his will. The Don Juan, or Seductive Boy, flirts with both self-contempt and other-centered contempt. He is often nurturing and weak, gentle and subtly abusive. Each style can be combined with aspects of the other two, so the possibilities are complex and subtle. These statements are a brief overview of a man's contemptuous style of relating.

6. Consider these attitudes that often lie behind each style. Which of these do you suspect might be behind your relational style?

The Nice Boy

_____ I place a high priority on being liked by other people.

_____ One of my main goals is to keep peace and avoid conflict with other people.

_____ I feel a lot of contempt for myself, but I try not to let others know about that.

_____ I'd rather not make decisions.

_____ I let others make choices so that I am not responsible for what happens.

_____ Sexual passion scares me.

_____ People would be surprised if they knew how angry I am.

_____ I tend to let a woman make the first move in a relationship, especially in the sexual sphere.

_____ I am rarely confronted because I am so kind.

_____ A lot more women than men consider me to be their friend.

_____ I rarely lose my temper.

_____ I have trouble standing up to aggressive people or evildoers.

_____ I think people find me pleasant.

_____ I feel lonely.

_____ I don't like to impose on other people.

_____ I am not good at delegating tasks to others.

_____ I have trouble saying no.

_____ I feel inadequate a lot of the time.

The Macho Boy
_____ I see myself as a take-charge, task-oriented person.

_____ I hate to be dependent on people.

_____ I tend to be indifferent to the feelings of others.

_____ I am often cynical and suspicious.

_____ I usually feel anger when other people might feel sadness or fear.

> "Throughout my adolescence I viewed women as the way to establish and prove my masculinity. My objective was not to love a woman; rather, I desired to have sexual relations so that I could prove that I was adequate and normal as a man."

_____ I can usually tell when people are being dishonest or untrustworthy.

_____ I don't put much stock in positive feedback.

_____ I like to be in charge.

_____ When challenged, I am willing to go toe to toe with anyone to accomplish what I think is right.

_____ I lose my temper fairly frequently.

_____ I am often too busy for sex; but when I feel sexual, I expect my wife to comply.

_____ I require my partner to be sexually satisfied.

_____ My wife would say she feels a lot of pressure to perform to my expectations.

_____ People value me for my competence.

_____ I am known as a person with strong opinions.

_____ Nobody would think of me as usually warm or gentle.

_____ When I feel threatened or angry, I tend to be verbally aggressive or sarcastic to intimidate the other person.

_____ I can be pleasant and generous; but people know they'll be sorry if they cross my line.

The Seductive Boy

_____ I really like a good time.

_____ People would consider me smooth.

_____ I can get out of trouble almost every time.

_____ I can convince others of almost anything.

_____ You can count on me to be unpredictable.

_____ I have moderate or wild mood swings.

_____ I take things out of context or mishear them.

_____ I am weak sometimes and bold at other times.

_____ I'm not good at keeping long-term relationships.

_____ When a relationship starts to get too close, I want to end it so I . . .

   _____ retreat.

   _____ cause conflict.

   _____ do something disloyal.

   _____ get attracted to another woman.

   _____ Other (name it):

_____ I use money and gifts to endear others to me.

_____ Women often want to rescue and mother me.

_____ I draw women into my control.

_____ Once I sexually use a woman, I quickly lose interest.

We did not include a questionnaire for men to give to friends because it's even harder for men to take such a step of vulnerability than it is for women. If you're motivated, you could put together a questionnaire yourself, based on the items in question 6.

****

7. Based on what you've learned about yourself in chapters 4 through 10, how would you summarize your style of relating to each of the following?

YOURSELF

MEN

WOMEN

8. How do you feel when you think about what you have learned in questions 1 through 7? What does this information make you feel like doing?

9. What is your typical way of responding when you are confronted with something negative about yourself?

10. What would you like to say to God right now?

LACKING BONES[1]
by Karen C. Lee-Thorp

Lacking bones, a crustacean needs a hard shell.
    Lady Lobster
    She knows the meat inside her is tender,
        tasty.
    All around her, predators linger to devour.
    And her shell,
        though hard enough to frustrate idle poking,
        is brittle,
        giving shape to her otherwise formless flesh
        but too fragile to withstand concerted attack.
Therefore, she has claws.

Who can wave a magic wand
        causing slivers of bone to grow where there were no slivers
        deep in her soul?
    The slivers join and grow, pushing their hard, sharp tips
        throughout her flesh.
    A thousand knives.
    But one day, the slivers will be a skeleton,
        smooth, rounded bone upon bone.
    The shell will be unneeded,
like the claws.

Lacking bones, a mollusk needs a hard shell.
    Who has the power
    to change a lobster to a lady, a mussel to a man?

NOTE

1. Karen C. Lee-Thorp, "Lacking Bones," previously unpublished poem, used by permission.

CHAPTER ELEVEN

REPENTANCE

What Is Repentance?

The route to change has begun in the long trek through the swamps of honesty—honesty about the damage we have suffered and the unloving ways we have chosen to protect ourselves from further pain. We have trudged through stunned shock that "it" could really be true; rage at ourselves, others, and God; and the empty question of despair: "What use is there in dealing with any of this?"

We reach drier ground that signals the swamps are thinning out. From here, the road splits. One fork heads left along level ground out to the edge of the swamp and then back around to an even deeper denial: "This is too much; I refuse to suffer over this anymore." That highway leads to plastic functioning, a parody of life. The other fork is a rocky path into foothills of grief over the damage of the abuse and our stubborn responses to it. Sorrow begins to melt our hatred toward ourselves and others.

Again the way divides. We can wander the angry forests of penance, building a case against our abusers, the wicked world, and the God who failed to intervene. We can pass the rest of our lives there independent of the world and the God we struggle with. Or, we can set out on the long climb up the crag of repentance, crying out to God with our whole being for the power to live for Him.

The word *repentance* tends to conjure up images of a gaunt man in black pointing a bony finger and bellowing, "Repent, sinner!" And the trouble with erasing this image is that it's hard to come up with an accurate one that is drawn so clearly. The basic sense of the word is changing direction, turning away from sin and toward God. Repentance is not merely a decision of the will to do right instead of wrong. At its deepest level, "it is *an internal shift in our perceived source of life*. It is recognizing that our self-protective means to avoid hurt have not ushered us into real living (the reckless abandon to God that ultimately leads to a deep sense of wholeness and joy) or to purposeful, powerful relating. Repentance is the process of deeply acknowledging the supreme call to love, which is violated at every moment, in every relationship—a law that

> "Repentance—it's painful, I love it, it surprises me, and I don't understand it at all. How's that for ambivalence! I try to do it but I can't, then it happens by the grace of God. I've seen repentance in some areas and don't know if it will ever come in others. . . . When I get on a roll with contempt and I can't get out of it for days, it seems like I'll never understand repentance."

applies even to those who have been heinously victimized. . . . Love silences explanation, penetrates excuses, and humbles the heart, preparing that heart to be captured by the gospel of grace. Ultimately, repentance is a humble, broken return to God" (*The Wounded Heart*, pages 217-218).

But there's a catch: We are utterly unable to do that. Repentance is not something we can decide to do and then do; it is something God works in us. Then what's our part? Our part is getting ourselves ready for God to work repentance in us. Before God can turn us, we have to become deeply dissatisfied with the way things are now, desperately hungry for change, and hopeful that change is possible. When we find ourselves caught in a wrong behavior or attitude, it's pointless merely to decide to do better. But just leaving the ball in God's court is to avoid our responsibility. Our job is to ask and keep asking the question, *What is blocking me from the desperate hunger to change and the excited hope that it can happen?* What are we still getting out of this habit? Why don't we think the loving way would be richer? Why do we doubt God can change us?

Read pages 215-233 of *The Wounded Heart*, which explain more fully what repentance is and isn't. Note clearly for the hundredth time that God does not call you to repent for the abuse or for what you experienced in it.

1. Working through the previous ten chapters should have brought you to some set-tled convictions about your situation. Putting the truth in plain terms can be a great help in preventing denial from seeping back in through cracks in your floor. Check the statements you believe are true about yourself.

_____ I have been abused.

_____ I am a victim of a crime against my body and soul.

_____ As a victim, I am not in any way responsible for the crime, no matter what I might have experienced or gained as a result of the abuse.

_____ Abuse has damaged my soul.

_____ The damage is due to the interweaving dynamics of powerlessness, betrayal, and ambivalence.

_____ My damage is different from others' in extent, intensity, and consequences, but it is worthy to be addressed and worked through no matter what occurred.

_____ It will take time to deal with internal wounds; the process must not be hurried.

_____ I must not keep a veil of secrecy and shame over my past; but I am not required to share my past with anyone I feel is untrustworthy or insensitive.

2. What have been the hardest aspects of honesty for you? Which of the above or other truths about your abuse and its effects have you found hard to see, face, or believe? In other words, in what areas are you most tempted to slip back to denial?

Penance

A caution is in order. It's tempting to become frustrated with ourselves whenever we find we can't just decide to shift our perceived source of life. It's easy to slide from repentance into penance. True repentance admits helplessness: We really are totally unable in ourselves to make that shift. Penance, in contrast, presumes we are able to make amends on our own. We set about changing our behavior. We think that when we've asked for forgiveness, that should be the end of the matter. Repentance softens us with a humble plea for undeserved mercy. Penance hardens us with a self-satisfied certainty that we've paid our debts and we owe nothing more.

Oddly enough, violent tears of self-pity ("I feel so bad about this, I'm so bad . . .") can often be an attempt to pay for one's sin with emotional flogging. After such a show of grief, how could anyone raise the subject again or ask for more substantial change? Again, self-contempt is counterfeit conviction and evades repentance.

But we're so accustomed to self-contempt that when we begin to look at all repentance requires, we can easily say, "I'm so bad. I fall so short of this standard that I'll never make it. It probably isn't even worth thinking about it, let alone trying it." This is an extremely effective dodge. If you like, make a large check mark in the margin every time you say something similar to yourself while working through this and the next chapter.

The fruit that comes from the internal shift of true repentance will include at least these three elements: (1) a refusal to be dead, (2) a refusal to mistrust, and (3) a refusal to despise passion. Each refusal must finally be energized by a realization that offering all that we are in the service of others is the essence of life.

A Refusal to Be Dead

"In essence, the choice to be dead is the choice to turn one's back on the Author of life, to deny Him the opportunity to touch our lives deeply and to use us fully according to His good purposes" (*The Wounded Heart*, page 223).

3. What reasons make deadness an attractive option for you even now? (You may want to reread pages 223-228 of *The Wounded Heart*.)

> "I realize [repentance] is not thinking of myself as bad and trying harder to do better. It is dealing with my own will to make life work apart from God as that plays out in my life. It is dealing with my deepest pain and at that moment realizing if it were not for God's grace to me, I deserve to be consumed as well as my abuser."

4. What are some things you have typically done to deaden yourself?

> *Watching television.*
> *Working.*
> *Sending my mind into a fantasy world.*

5. Sadness has to do with disappointment over current losses. About what have you felt sad in the past week or so? What kinds of things spark sadness in you?

6. Grief is an intense feeling of sadness about a loss that cannot be regained or replaced. What deeply important things have you lost that cannot be replaced and require grieving?

> *I never even had a chance to save my virginity for my husband.*
> *My marriage fell apart because of these abuse issues; and I didn't understand it then.*

7. How easily does grief come when you think about these losses? What seems to get in the way?

8. In biblical times, people acted out their grief: tearing their clothes, putting ashes on their heads, breaking a bowl, playing special music, wailing. What would help you to express your grief? (Does it help you to talk to someone, cry, play special music, tear up an old sheet?)

9. Once we have begun grieving our losses, we can move on to sorrow over the ways we've damaged others or failed to love them with our ways of protecting ourselves from hurt. Who have you damaged because you felt you had to protect yourself rather than rely on God's grace? How have you damaged them?

Answering this question could take some time. Take all the time you need, understanding that you could never come up with a perfectly complete record. Utter completeness is less important than honestly confronting yourself with some of the serious damage you've done.

> *I never let my college roommates see what an alive follower of Christ could be like. My example certainly didn't make Christ attractive to them, and I never even cared to enter into the pain of the struggles they were going through. I was too dead to love them; I was just existing and surviving. I've denied my husband the joy of a passionate, tender wife. I've been a dutiful wife who has made it easy for him to avoid intimacy.*

"One of two questions that I use as my mainstay is simply, 'What does repentance look like for me in this situation?' Maybe it's deciding *not* to volunteer for another committee. Perhaps it's 'wasting' money on some sexy underwear that no one will ever see but me."

> *We exult in our tribulations, knowing that tribulation brings about perseverance; and perseverance proven character; and proven character, hope; and hope does not disappoint because the love of God has been poured out within our hearts through the Holy Spirit. (Romans 5:3)*

The reason we want to be overcome by an addictive substance or behavior is that addiction ends sorrow. If we are alive to the pain of tribulation, we have an opportunity to persevere and acquire proven character. We will have more love and care to give away to others. But this process of sorrow is cut short when we immerse ourselves in a method of medicating the sorrows we are faced with.

10. Think about the addictions you identified in chapters 2 and 7, or other addictions you've become aware of. How have they served to deaden pain and sorrow in your life?

11. How do you feel about what you've written in questions 9 and 10? (Check as many as apply.)

____ I feel bad about myself. I feel confirmed that I really am a corrupt person and a failure in relationships. (Self-contempt.)

____ I don't blame myself because I know I did those things because I was damaged by abuse. I was doing the best I could.

____ I feel sorrow for the damage these people have suffered; I know what it's like to be damaged by someone who is incapable of deep love.

____ I need to look for ways to make it up to as many of these people as possible.

____ I feel ashamed that I have let God down.

____ It grieves me to know that I've wounded God repeatedly.

____ It's painful to know there's nothing I can do to fix what I've done.

____ I'm so grateful that God values and delights in me even though He knows I can't make up for the damage I've caused.

____ I'm relieved that I've confessed those sins and I can forget about them.

____ I feel determined not to do those things any more.

____ Other (name it):

12. Few of us find that deep grief and sorrow unto life come quickly and easily. Many things having to do with shame, self-contempt, powerlessness, betrayal, and ambivalence block these feelings. What are some issues that still feel shameful to you regarding your abuse or its effects?

A Refusal to Mistrust

"The opposite of mistrust is not trust, but *care*. When we view a person with mistrust, it is as if their life no longer matters. We 'write them off.' Mistrust prejudges their every word and deed so they can never reach our heart. A protective shield descends whenever we're around them, and relationship is severed. . . . Repentance, or a refusal to mistrust, reengages the God-given desire to care, to be kind, to comfort, and to be concerned about the temporal and eternal destiny of those who have harmed us.

"A refusal to mistrust, however, is neither gullible nor stupid. . . . Insipid, naive trust is not a commitment to care; it is denial designed to alleviate the need to be fully engaged in relationship" (*The Wounded Heart*, pages 226-227).

13. What is your typical way(s) of showing mistrust?

> "My repentance shows up when I *ask* in relationships—as I let people know I can be hurt, and that I need them and am not a tower of strength. I had to learn how to let people fail me in the context of wanting. Before I had no problem if they didn't come through—I never wanted! I have had to begin learning how to live with a sorrow of never having enough and to let it tenderize me, not harden me. My attitude toward my hurting is very different. I almost feel it works for me now, instead of crippling me."

_____ I make my coolness, disdain, or suspicion obvious.

_____ I naively trust people with money, information, even obedience, but I don't offer my soul or care enough to challenge someone's harmful actions.

_____ I'm friendly, even playful, with people, but I keep me moving and them spinning so they can't get at my heart.

_____ Other (name it):

14. Consider the process of sadness, grief, and sorrow described on pages 228 of *The Wounded Heart*. What are some of your key past and current relationships about which you feel deeply betrayed?

15. How would you describe the cost you've paid and will continue to pay? What are the irretrievable losses that can only be grieved?

16. How have you damaged others by your mistrust?

"I have been more effective in admitting my weaknesses and talking about struggles. It is easy in a large group or from a platform; harder one to one because I lose control. One to one, the blush can be seen, questions can be asked, I can be pursued. I make a conscious effort to allow this as part of my recovery. I am very aware when I fail. I walk away, and realize, 'I did it again.' I hid my heart."

17. How do you feel when you contemplate that damage?

18. How are you seeing God these days? Do you see Him as a games player, a cosmic sadist who uses pleasure to entice then pain to frustrate His victims, or as someone to placate and ignore or disdainfully despise? Do you think He is trustworthy?

A Refusal to Despise Passion

"Passion can be defined as *the deep response of the soul to life: the freedom to rejoice and to weep*. One of the most difficult commands to fulfill is to 'weep with those who weep and rejoice with those who rejoice' (Romans 12:15). It requires open-hearted, other-centered, reckless involvement. Passion is tasting pleasure with delight, brokenness with tears, and evil with hatred" (*The Wounded Heart*, page 229).

19. How do you show your tendency to despise passion?

_____ I try to keep myself from being too pleased with success or compliments.

_____ I feel ashamed of my sexual desires.

_____ I don't want to feel how deeply disappointed I am with the way my husband treats me.

_____ I've had the hardest time admitting to myself that I really hate someone.

_____ I have trouble being warmly affectionate with my friends/family.

_____ I hate dissolving in tears in front of people (or alone).

_____ I have trouble letting go and really playing or being silly.

_____ I don't want people to think I'm wild, weird, or sexually loose.

_____ I'm highly emotional, but I avoid getting attached to anyone or anything.

_____ Other (name it):

20. What losses have you suffered because you have been unable to be unself-conscious, spontaneous, and unashamed in your physical and emotional responses to life? What could you have had if you were free to be passionate?

> "Learning about sexual abuse brought hope and freedom for me and opened new categories for understanding my difficulties in forming intimate relationships with women. Looking back, I realize that I used the sexual abuse experiences to explain why I felt empty, lonely, and flawed and as an excuse to keep from having to emotionally involve myself with a woman—something I know I am capable of but deeply fear."

21. What damage have you done to others because you have refused to be passionate?

For Group Discussion

First discuss what *repentance* means, and how it differs from *penance*. Try to help each person in the group grasp the difference. How do you feel about the idea of repentance in these terms?

You'll probably want to move through this chapter question by question, if you have time. Encourage group members who feel far from grief and sorrow—growth is a process and no one is required to grow as fast as anyone else. Watch for tendencies to slip into penance, into thinking you have to change by your own willpower.

Be sure to save time for question 21. You may be able to help each other figure out what repentance might look like in your lives.

Talk to God about where you are in the journey toward repentance. Tell Him where you are feeling grief or sorrow, and where you aren't Tell Him how you feel about yourself and Him.

22. Read pages 230-233 in *The Wounded Heart* with your own style of relating in mind. What would be two or three ways in which repentance might manifest itself in your life?

"Repentance for me that day involved returning some beige door paint in exchange for what seemed risky and racy, black and red, and exchanging marigolds for twenty-four pots (so they could be perfectly groomed together) for twenty-four *different* plants, each in a different color, each a different kind. It may not seem like a big deal, but I get excited now just thinking about how extreme that seemed at the time and how alive I felt as I did that."

"Repentance is facing what is true: 'I am a sinner and double-minded, and I deserve to be separated from God.' *It is a shift in perspective as to where life is found.* It is a deep recognition that life comes only to the broken, desperate, dependent hearts that longs for God. It is a melting into the warm arms of God, acknowledging the wonder of being received when it would be so understandable to be spurned. It is taking our place at the great feast, eating to our fill, and delighting in the undeserved party being held in honor of our return" (*The Wounded Heart*, page 233).

23. Write a letter to God, telling Him how you are feeling about your situation and Him right now. Is "melting into the warm arms of God" possible for you yet? What gets in the way? Just talk to Him honestly about where you feel you are in the process of repentance.

24. To portray your unique directions for repentance, try making two collages:

• My Deadness (or mistrust, or hatred of passion)
• My Refusal to be Dead

Cut out pictures and words from magazines that express what deadness is like for you. Then find ones that depict what you would be like if you turned away from deadness.

CHAPTER TWELVE

BOLD LOVE

This could be a frustrating chapter. If you are just beginning to work on honesty and are barely wetting your toes in the icy waters of repentance, even thinking about boldly loving those who have harmed you may seem as absurd as sprouting wings and flying. If this is your situation, we hope you will treat yourself gently in this chapter. Remember to draw large check marks in the margin each time you find yourself saying, "It's impossible"; "I'm so stupid"; or "I should be able to do better."

What Is Love?

Repentance may be the second least-understood word in Christian jargon; *love* is surely the first. Love is not an absence of anger—God is furious at the corruption in us and what it has done to us precisely because He loves us passionately. Love does not minimize or forget past harm—that is nearly always unbiblical denial. Finally, love is not pious other-centeredness that is devoid of pleasure for the giver—the Apostle Paul clearly felt great when his loving efforts bore fruit, and he was not ashamed to admit he was doing it all for the rewards of heaven.

Read pages 235-255 of *The Wounded Heart*.

"Love can be defined as *the free gift that voluntarily cancels the debt in order to free the debtor to become what he might be if he experiences the joy of restoration*" (*The Wounded Heart*, page 239). This definition insists that *forgiveness* is an essential part of love. But the idea of victims forgiving abusers is repulsive to many sensible people for some very good reasons. It's nauseating to kiss and make up while the abuser goes on exploiting us and other victims. Yet biblical forgiveness is not the kind that pretends everything is all right and invites more misuse, but one that involves a hunger for *restoration*, *bold love*, and *revoked revenge*. A closer look at these elements should make the idea of wise, biblical forgiveness not only palatable but liberating.

First, however, it's important to understand that true forgiveness is part of the healing process and so is not possible until we have faced the damage of powerlessness, ambivalence, and betrayal, and have begun to repent from deadness, mistrust, and the hatred of passion. We needn't feel pushed by other people or our own sense of having to be righteous. Forcing forgiveness before its time will produce only more shame, contempt, and denial of the true state of our hearts.

A caveat: Be aware that if you have only recently recovered memories of sexual abuse, you *may* be mistaken. Memory is a tricky thing, and to be falsely accused of a crime as heinous as sexual abuse is an agonizing experience. So before you voice an accusation, do whatever you can to verify your new memories with other family members or any source available to you. The material in this chapter assumes you have good reason to believe you were abused by a specific person.

Hunger for Restoration

How could we possibly hunger to have intimate relationship with someone who has so evilly betrayed intimacy with us before? Certainly we would be masochists to want relationship with a wicked person. God agrees; He has no intention of letting wicked people live in His eternal Kingdom either. God longs to be reconciled not with us as we are in our self-centered rebellion, but as the loving, radiant people He intends to turn us into. His clear vision of what we can become in Christ is what drives both His tender care for our woundedness and His relentless assault on our self-protectiveness.

Likewise, as we begin to taste the joy of our own restoration with God, we can begin to hunger for relationship not with the abuser as he is, but as he could be if he allowed God to transform him. We can ask God to show us our abuser as he would be in Christ: the hard shell softened, the cutting voice gentle but ringing with joyful authority, the dead eyes bright with compassion. We know such a total transformation is impossible, but no more impossible than what God is already doing in us. Gradually we begin to hate the evil that grips our abuser because it blocks the glorious impossibility we have glimpsed in him.

Hungering for restoration is not the same as offering it. Jesus told His disciples, "If your brother sins, rebuke him, and if he repents, forgive him" (Luke 17:3). As we become committed to seeing that glorious impossibility become possible, our first step may be to rebuke the abuser, hoping against hope that he will repent so we can forgive him and restore relationship. But if he refuses to repent, we are left hungering and hoping (not stalking away in contempt) but offering nothing. We cannot give him access to our heart until we see signs of repentance.

1. Which of the following would you choose?

____ That God would totally destroy your abuser(s) so that not a molecule of his being continued to exist.

____ That God would totally restore him to be the person God designed him to be.

2. a. What does contemplating this choice cause you to feel?

b. What do you feel like doing?

3. If you can, explain why you made the choice you did in question 1.

Bold Love

"Bold love is a commitment to do whatever it takes (apart from sin) to bring health (salvation) to the abuser. . . . *Love is a powerful force and energy to reclaim the potential good in another, even at the risk of great sacrifice and loss*" (*The Wounded Heart*, page 241).

When we catch the vision of what someone can become, we can become eager to help the transformation take place.

> The load, or weight, or burden of my neighbor's glory should be laid on my back, a load so heavy that only humility can carry it, and the backs of the proud will be broken. It is a serious thing to live in a society of potential gods and goddesses, to remember that the dullest and most uninteresting person you talk to may one day be a creature which, if you saw it now, you would be strongly tempted to worship or else a horror and a corruption such as you now meet, if at all, only in a nightmare. All day long we are, in some degree, helping each other to one or other of these destinations.[1]

To love boldly, then, is to see a person's deficiencies without denial and at the same time imagine how he would be so different if God changed him. It's no good making up a picture of how *we'd* like the person to be (that would be arrogant and controlling); we must pray to be shown God's intentions. Then, when we have some idea of what God wants, we can pray for that to happen with integrity. We can also ask God to show us our part in bringing the glory about.

4. What might your abuser(s) be like if he became what God made him to be? Ask God to show you something of the possibilities, then jot down your thoughts.

5. How do you feel when you think about helping to make this person glorious instead of hideous?

Revoking Revenge

"The desire to do harm to another is not always the same as wanting him to pay for his sin. Many times I have prayed for harm to come to a blind, arrogant, harmful man or woman in order to bring them to their senses. Paul encourages us to pour burning coals on an evildoer's head rather than strike back in revenge. John Stott argues that 'pouring burning coals' is a New Testament metaphor for shaming or causing embarrassment. . . .

"There are three important components that separate a hunger for justice from fantasies or actions of revenge. First, revenge leaves no room for restoration. The judgment is final. . . . Second, revenge gets in the way of God. Our acts of revenge are puny; His are perfect. Paul does not condemn the Romans for *wanting* revenge, only for *seeking* it. . . . Finally, God gives an opportunity for conquering and overcoming evil today: Do good" (*The Wounded Heart*, pages 243-244).

We tend to read the Bible's references to the judgment of the wicked with some embarrassment. We feel that good, compassionate Christians ought not cheer at passages like this one:

> *I saw an angel standing in the sun, who cried in a loud voice to all the birds flying in midair, "Come, gather together for the great supper of God, so that you may eat the flesh of kings, generals, and mighty men, of horses and their riders, and the flesh of all people, free and slave, small and great."*
>
> *Then I saw the beast and the kings of the earth and their armies gathered together to make war against the rider on the horse and his army. but the beast was captured, and with him the false prophet who had performed the miraculous signs on his behalf. . . . The two of them were thrown alive into the fiery lake of burning sulfur. The rest of them were killed with the sword that came out of the mouth of the rider on the horse, and all the birds gorged themselves on their flesh. (Revelation 19:17-18)*

By contrast, the biblical writers recorded such scenes with unashamed gusto. They never pretended they wanted anything for their enemies other than that they be either totally transformed or torn into shreds.

6. In passages like Isaiah 24 and the previous one from Revelation, God seems to look forward to the day when He will crush the evil one and his followers. What do you think about making the wicked pay permanently for their deeds? What do you think about a God who is looking forward to the day of reckoning?

7. Think about setting aside your desire for immediate revenge and counting on God's future, thorough revenge. (You might reread pages 243-244 of *The Wounded Heart*.) What does revoking revenge seem to you—crazy, unthinkable, terrific? Why?

8. What does a person have to believe about God for revoking revenge to even begin to sound rational?

Doing genuine good to an evil person is the best attack on evil. Genuine good doesn't mean doing what the person wants or playing nice to avoid conflict. Rather, it means responding to his true physical or other needs. Treating an enemy with strong kindness can shock him into a shame that can lead to repentance.

9. What might revoking revenge look like in one relationship you are currently facing? How could you encourage shame and repentance in that person by responding to a true need with aliveness, kindness, and passion?

Loving Your Enemy

It's important to approach different kinds of abusers differently.

Average Abusers

10. Who are some of your "average" abusers (pages 245-247 of *The Wounded Heart*)?

11. What are some of the abusive things you have had to endure from those people?

Loving an average abuser involves:

- •Setting boundaries, where appropriate (these depend on one's typical style of relating).
- •Offering kindness, where appropriate.
- •Grinning and bearing the situation of a sinful world.
- •Continuing to move toward the qualities of the soul (such as patience and gentleness) that are not lost in the midst of pain and conflict.

"The issue is not 'What is the right thing to do?' but, 'What will give us a greater opportunity to love?' . . . Boundaries always serve to enhance relationships. . . . For that reason, no detailed picture will ever capture what it means to love another average abuser. It must rest in the heart of the lover, whose soul is warmed by the gospel, whose imagination is set free by repentance, whose hands are free to serve and mouth free to rebuke" (*The Wounded Heart*, page 247).

12. Choose one average abusive situation you are facing or have recently faced. What might be a creative way to respond in love? How can you help draw the person(s) in question toward goodness? What would be appropriate boundaries and/or kindness? Where do grin-and-bear-it and improving your character fit in?

(If you threw up your hands in despair, put a large check mark in the margin. You may want to ask a friend to help you brainstorm.)

Abuser Surrogates

An abuser surrogate is a person with whom you intensely replay your past damage and self-protection, usually your most intimate relationship (theoretically or actually).

13. Who (if anyone) is your abuser surrogate (pages 247-249)? You may have more than one.

14. What are some of the things this person does to replay your damage?

15. What are some ways you replay your self-protective strategies with this person?

Loving an abuser surrogate includes:

- Building consistent boundaries.
- Deepening intimacy.
- Learning to sorrow and rejoice.
- Persevering in faith toward God's redemption of this person as someone clothed in dignity and strength.

16. What might be some boundaries you could set with your abuser surrogate that would *enhance* your relationship?

17. In what ways could you pursue deeper intimacy with this person, without violating wise boundaries?

18. How do you feel about doing that? Consider: What might it cost you? What would have to happen in you for you even to be able to do this?

Capital-A Abuser(s)

19. Who would you put in the category of capital-A Abuser(s), past and present (pages 249-255)?

"Loving the capital-A offender sometimes involves confronting him. The victim should carefully consider her motives. . . . There are two: concern for the abuser and concern for those he may still be abusing" (*The Wounded Heart*, page 250).
    Confrontation is a process. It includes:

•Building consistent boundaries.
•Rebuking and inviting the abuser to repent.
•Offering relationship.
•Deepening intimacy.
•Learning to sorrow and rejoice.
•Persevering in God's redemption of the abuser.

"Before the victim attempts to directly rebuke her abuser and invite him to repent, she should have made substantial shifts in the style of relating she has habitually used to distance herself and seek revenge against him and others" (*The Wounded Heart*, page 251).

20. What do you think would have to change in the way you relate before you could confront your abuser? (Or do you think you're ready now?) How will you have to change inside before confrontation can be constructive?

21. What factors make you desire a restored relationship with your abuser?

22. What makes you *not* desire a restored relationship?

23. What makes you *hopeful* that restoration might be possible?

24. On the other hand, what makes you *doubt* it will ever happen?

> "Today I said goodbye to T. I told him I liked him. What a gross understatement. Did he know what was behind those words 'I like you'? Did he have any idea what courage it took to say them so clearly, without flinching? I can't remember if I told him that the first time I ever told D I loved him was only a month ago—after twenty-two years of marriage!"

25. Given where you are in the process of repentance and where your abuser is, what do you believe should be your next step in dealing with him or her? (Are there boundaries to set? Should you concentrate on your own repentance awhile? Do you need to change the way you relate to your abuser?)

26. How are you feeling right now? What do you feel like doing?

Taking Stock

If you've worked all the way through this workbook (even if you've skipped some sections), you've completed a major undertaking. You may feel a sense of accomplishment; but it's more likely that you feel some anticlimax, a bit of a letdown. After all, you've put in a lot of work and suffered all kinds of anguish, and (unless you're very unusual) you're still screwed up.

So what's next? Where to now? Do the workbook again? It begins to be painfully clear that you'll be screwed up forever. But even if you don't feel much more healed or much more loving, healing and loving aren't the bottom line. Is God more of a friend than He seemed when you began this workbook? If so, it's been worth it.

That doesn't solve your problem of what to do next, of course. It will probably be helpful to determine where you are now, just as you did at the beginning. Knowing where you are now should help you decide where you want to go.

27. Look back at the first question you answered in this workbook: question 1 on pages 13-15 of this workbook. In what ways would your answers now be the same? In what ways would they be different?

28. Look at your goals in using this workbook—question 4 on page 16. How have you fared at reaching those goals for your relationships with each of the following?

YOURSELF

OTHERS

GOD

"Life now is harder in many ways. . . . My hunger for relationship is felt so much more intensely now, and I really desire to have quality relationships in my 'real world' everyday life. My greatest temptation is to try to stay with the status quo, on auto-pilot for the next two months when I plan to move. . . . Whether I'll let some trustworthy men and women here see me as I am . . . is something that I still don't know. I know that I want to. As my hunger for that kind of relationship has intensified, so have the attempts to kill the hunger through contemptuous behaviors . . . but there is a difference now. I think I experience (on more than an intellectual plane, as I did before), the futility of those behaviors to touch the deep parts of my soul, to even come close to satisfying. I thought recently in the midst of some of that contemptuous behavior toward myself, 'This just isn't me. I don't have the heart for punishing myself like this anymore.' I sensed my loveliness even in the midst of my sin. I knew then that some of the change that had taken place . . . was lasting and substantial."

29. Are there a few things you've faced that have really begun to change you? Ask some friends who've been with you in the process. What do they notice is different about you?

30. Look over the collages, drawings, etc., you've made as you've moved through this workbook. How would a picture of your life now be different from when you began this process?

31. a. Are you more inclined now to seek counseling from a professional, or less? If you're thinking about doing this, what might be your goals?

b. What questions would you ask a therapist, to determine if he or she would be helpful to you?

32. Where would you like to go from here? During the next year, what changes would you like to see in the way you relate to each of these?

YOURSELF

OTHERS

For Group Discussion

Imagine a large and lovely tree, a tree that invites creatures to come and nest. A tree whose leafy arms hold the promise of comfort and rest. A person who is a shelter is one who affords those that enter her life the joy of relaxing in her love. She has come alive to her longings and the beauty of offering her soul without contempt or pressured performing. This aliveness is not a fruit that she uses to adorn herself. Rather, it is for the explicit purpose of having more to give to others for their well-being and to God for His glory.

There is beauty in giving shelter. The path to being inviting is (1) to enjoy being soft as a woman, (2) to enjoy a deepened capacity to respond to others from the soul, and (3) to enjoy the substance within you that allows you to make difficult and unpopular decisions.

1. Name five traits of people you know whom you consider to be sheltering trees.

2. What role does prayer, journaling, Bible study, or commitment to others play in the development of those people's strength?

3. What has enticed you within this group to want to become a sheltering tree for others?

4. Briefly tell one group member about how you've enjoyed in him or her one of the traits of a sheltering tree.

5. Draw a sheltering tree. Label the branches with things you have learned through this workbook that will support your being soft, bold, or strong. Share these with the group.

> "I was really thrown for a loop. I was not prepared for the fact that as I allowed that little girl to grieve and grow up, this woman would feel more and have a depth to her she had never known or experienced. So when I blew it in a big way (the depth of my sin) one day, I felt a greater shame and contempt than I had ever known. I was furious. Angry that I ever started the process, angry that God had not freed me from this, angry at myself because I was incapable of change.
>
> "I realized during that that I wanted to be sinless. . . . That there would be no more shame, no more contempt, no more blunders. Understanding the process of sanctification has been eye opening. . . .
>
> "I am more relaxed now as God woos me and puts me through the fire. I am more relaxed because He is There. I look forward to relaxing more with others, too. I am not there."

GOD

33. a. What might be your next step toward reaching those goals?

b. How does God fit into this process?

> *"Now have come the salvation and the power and the kingdom of our God,*
>   *and the authority of his Christ.*
> *For the accuser of our brothers,*
>   *who accuses them before our God day and night,*
>   *has been hurled down.*
> *They overcame him*
>   *by the blood of the Lamb*
>   *and by the word of their testimony;*
> *they did not love their lives so much as to shrink from death." (Revelation 12:10-11)*

NOTE

1. C. S. Lewis, *The Weight of Glory* (Grand Rapids, MI: W. B. Eerdmans Publishing Co., 1977), pages 14-15.

For Group Discussion

Plan something fun to do together to celebrate completing this group experience. Have a dinner, a party, or something active like a skating trip. You'll also want to discuss where each of you is and what you might do next, but ending a discussion like that and just walking away would be sad.

Plan time in your final discussion to evaluate the group experience. What did you like? What would you do differently next time?

A NOTE TO GROUP MEMBERS

A powerful yet fragile gift from God is wrapped up in the people in your group. It is essential to be connected to people while you take this journey into the past and present effects of your abuse. It is essential, not just because you will need support along the way, but also because you have so much to give. As you know from *The Wounded Heart*, the essence of life is giving, not getting. As you enter the group experience, remember that talking about pain is never more of a priority than loving others. In some ways the message you convey to a member of the group may be the reason she goes forward to develop her gifts to bless her family and the Body of Christ.

If you look only to the leader for feedback, the rest of the group will get a crippling message: "You have nothing of value to give me." But if you are open to it, you will find as you plunge into grief that life-giving courage and laughter come from totally unexpected moments within your group. Each member will add to this life, and the incredible cycle of worship will begin. This is God's uncanny way of smiling as we create new patterns with our stories.

Imagine the crescendo of worship reflected in the stories you share. Perhaps in a few months you will look back on the weeks you were together as a group, and you will remember one act of love that seemed mundane at the time. Yet, it opened the heart of another member to her daughter. Her daughter felt the courage to grieve and renew her walk with God. Through this decision, a beauty was enhanced in her that challenged her husband. The stories go on and on, building ultimately to a song of worship that causes the Lord eternal joy. This is no ordinary support group!

IDEAS FOR GROUP LEADERS

If you're an old hand at leading support groups, you'll probably just skim this section. But if you're not, you may be eager for guidance. An excellent resource is Gerald Corey, et al., *Group Techniques*, second edition (Brooks Cole, 1992). Another is Neal F. McBride, *How to Lead Small Groups* (NavPress, 1990). You would be well advised to read at least one of these before launching your group. In addition, here are some thoughts to consider.

What Makes a Good Leader?

Behaviors Harmful to Group Process

Self-confessing. It is detrimental to use the group as a sounding board for your personal concerns. If you plan to teach about or express your opinion on matters unrelated to the group, consider another format, such as a class. In a support group, the important discoveries will come from the group members. Your self-disclosure should be kept at a minimum, except when you are telling your story. Disclosure seldom accomplishes as much as you hope; and it can stifle the disclosure of others.

Rescuing. It's tempting to reduce the tension of interactions by rescuing a group member. Many leaders respond to their own discomfort by choosing to intervene during conflicts, so that conflicts will never occur. In a sexual abuse group, this confirms the belief that deep realities cannot be faced and dealt with. Not all confrontations have a redemptive mood (see page 184). You will want to explore and deter any language or action that is abusive. But if a redemptive mood is present, the tension can be powerful. The healthy group can struggle through to a conclusion of the anger. The adults in your group may never have witnessed the resolution of a conflict. It may be foreign to them that you can face hard issues and yet continue to be "for" others in the group. The discovery that this is possible encourages participants to trust what they're made of. If you rescue them from conflict, you will solidify the perception that they are dangerous.

Positive Qualifications of a Leader

Gate-keeping. This involves making it possible for another member to make a contribution to the group, or suggesting limited talking time for everyone so that all will have a chance to be heard.

Standard-setting. It is often helpful for the leader to express standards for the group to use in choosing its content or procedures or in evaluating its decisions. You should describe and clarify reactions of the group to ideas or solutions. You are also responsible for setting the standard of acceptable ways of relating.

Consensus testing. You will want to ask tentatively for opinions in order to find out if the group is nearing consensus on its perception of an issue. Also ask for input so that a person's style of relating can be mirrored to him or her by the group. The leader sets a reflective tone.

Summarizing group feelings. Often the leader serves as an audience during group discussions. The participants will benefit from being allowed to relate apart from the leader. There will be times when the leader will summarize what group feelings seem to be. The leader might summarize different themes that have evolved through the meeting and draw conclusions about different points of view that have been expressed. The leader often interprets events and clarifies the significance of a here-and-now interaction.

Monitoring trust and confidentiality. The leader anticipates transitions or attitudes that have the potential to deteriorate the cohesiveness of the group. These include competition among members, absenteeism, subgrouping, a breach of confidentiality, and so on. The leader will be sensitive to the impact of adding new members to the group and will solicit feedback regarding any major change in the composition or scheduling of the group. Also, the leader will prepare the group for termination.

Planning Your Format

Opening Data Sheet
It is helpful for the leader to have an information sheet for each member in case of emergencies or changes in plans. This might include:

- Information about family
- Whom to contact in case of emergency
- Home and work phone numbers, with space for requesting no calls at work
- Facts on any previous counseling or group involvement

Exclusivity in Groups
Informative group with a totally revolving door. If your group is content-oriented— if its purpose is to convey information rather than to give participants a place to talk about their lives—then it's appropriate to keep membership in the group open. Participants may come occasionally, drop out, or join late without disrupting the group. A person may come with minimal commitment to attendance or openness to others. However, someone who wants to make only a minimal commitment might be better helped by simply reading and reflecting on the book *The Wounded Heart*. This workbook is designed for personal application and assumes some commitment to openness.

Stable group with a limited revolving door. If your group is a support group where members expect to deal directly with their personal histories, we recommend that you consider a closed group. This format allows a stable core of participants to develop trust, confidentiality, and a rich group process. If you find you have requests accumulating from prospective members, you can take these names on a waiting list and filter two new members in at a designated time after the first three months. If the waiting list grows to five or more names, begin a new group.

Factors to Consider

Attendance. Many groups find that trust is stronger when there is accountability with attendance. Obviously, there will be some scheduling conflicts, but it means a lot to the group if the member who will be absent contacts another member. As the group forges a trust that can sustain honesty, the facing of past abuse, and its aftermath, people need to know that they've disclosed these secrets to people who take the group seriously. Attendance need not be enforced with a military tone. It can merely be held up as a basic feature of groups that truly bond together.

Group size. We suggest that the group be no larger than ten, including two leaders. It is often helpful to have two leaders when challenging issues arise. Two leaders can also check each other's perceptions.

Time. Support group meetings usually need one and a half to two hours every week. The group should begin and end on time. There will be sessions when you are tempted to go overtime, but the short-term comfort of achieving closure will backfire in the long run. Participants need to know that as warm as the intimacy is within the group, it is not a family and it respects the needs of all to be able to make plans after the group. To attain a reasonable degree of closure, you can use the last ten minutes to summarize and clarify themes that have been covered during the session.

Overall length. The group should set a closure date. It is often helpful to run the group concurrently with the academic schedule of the public schools in your area. You will probably want to plan breaks around the holidays that all members will observe.

Age. Members should be above twenty years old. If you have requests from teenagers, a separate group should be started for them. This will enable the members to relate more directly as peers.

Attitudes to Encourage

Three attitudes can make a world of difference in your group's effectiveness. They have to do with confrontation, subgrouping, and confidentiality.

Confrontation

As you know from reading *The Wounded Heart*, people who attend a group on abuse will expect to discover things about their style of relating and many key areas of shame and contempt. (If those terms seem foreign to you because you have not yet read the book, don't worry. They'll make a lot more sense in a few weeks.) This group may be different from any other the members have joined. Probably few discipleship or Bible study groups have helped them see new things about their style of relating.

The desire to know and be known by others is to be commended. But although confrontation may seem fresh and exhilarating, it can be a great liability. When a group leader or member decides to mirror the impact of someone's words or behavior, he is taking atomic power and applying it. Will he be careful? Will the words be "according to the need of the moment"? There is a premium measure of the value of a confrontation: *Do the words offered carry a redemptive mood?*

In Acts 20:31, Paul says, "Remember that for three years I never stopped warning each of you day and night with tears." Paul had a three-year history with these folks! He knew something of loving with a redemptive mood.

When someone sees a failure in another group member, do you sense she has an internal quiet that allows her to wait, yearn for the other person, and pray about how and when to share her "sight"? It is a lot to ask, but nothing more than what love would ask. Recovery groups have no value unless the goal is maturing in love. Honesty will be an empty trophy if it becomes the goal of the group.

In Matthew 7:3-5 Jesus Christ spoke of examining the log in your own eye before confronting the speck in another's eye. Just as Paul cried out for those he confronted, Jesus outlined sacrifice as a prerequisite for confrontation.

Before someone confronts, does he know the costly priority of his own self-examination? Would the recipient of his words believe that the same energy he pours out for rebuke is also poured out on her behalf to see the truth planted, cultivated and harvested many weeks or years later? Helpful questions to ask ourselves are, "If I confront a group member's harm, am I prepared to be in relationship with her? Will I struggle toward the restoration of her beauty?"

This is the context that supports the weight of confrontation. A lighter frame, such as trying to end personal pain by confronting someone else, will collapse and do incredible harm to the entire group. The bridge of commitment is the only structure that can hold the weight of feedback.

What will you do if something said in the group is 100 percent accurate, but the speaker's heart is seeking revenge, authority, or any other motive that violates love? As leader, your job is to intercept such a comment. Can you intuit whether the speaker has weighed out her commitment to follow the words through with relationship? Here are two rules of thumb:

- *Does the confronter seek intimacy through intensity?* There are ways to be an extortionist. You gather some form of intimacy through the force of rapid self-disclosure or rapid confrontation.
- *Does the person confront with ease?* Does she lack deep reflection about her own life and the depth of relationship she will need to offer following the confrontation?

Subgrouping

Remember the cliques in high school? These smaller pairings of two or three people can disrupt a support group. The group will feel threatened if subgroups form and spend time together outside the group. (The same is true when leaders choose to give extra time to some members, but not all.) There's no point in banning subgroups as a hard and fast rule, but even if it is not mentioned directly, the rest of the group will sense if issues have been discussed between two group members outside the group. Hence, the group will be stronger if you can encourage the members to keep subgrouping to a minimum.

This attitude shows the greatest love and respect for the group: anything that took place outside the group is fair content that the group is free to discuss. There is no tone of exclusivity or secretive side discussions that must be kept out of the group's domain.

It is usually wise to plan a few group activities so that the group has a solid identity. Participants need to set aside the comfort they feel with certain other participants who seem more attractive or less threatening. Love sacrifices. These alliances can be postponed so that each member feels his contribution is valued.

Confidentiality

Proverbs 18:21 says, "The tongue has the power of life and death." The group will suffer an instant death blow if anything said or done in group is disclosed to someone outside the group. In the first few meetings, it will be important to underscore the covenant of confidentiality. You may want to have participants agree to this statement:

If I feel the need to process issues or feelings stirred up during the group meeting, I covenant to do this with another group member and/or my counselor, who is professionally committed to the same code of confidentiality.

Signature _____

Anonymity

Additionally, most groups follow a code of anonymity. They do not indicate to anyone outside the group the names of the other members. Why? Because this information gives the hearer a morsel to ponder: *"N must have been sexually abused."* Discuss anonymity with your group. What position do the members want to take?

Stages of Groups

Every group develops through stages on the road to becoming committed to bold love.

Stage One: Hesitant and Dependent

The decision to trust is based on the participants' confidence and attraction to the leader. Often they are hesitant to believe that the other members have anything of value to contribute to their situation. They will be dependent on the group leader. In the early stage of group relating, you will find that the members are constantly sizing up each other. They search for similarities and often give and receive advice. This "arm-chair counseling" will be obsolete later in the group. In stage one, it serves to lessen their awkwardness and is a vehicle for expressing mutual interest and caring. In other words, don't address it as a style-of-relating issue during the first week! It may be a conventional way of breaking the ice.

Stage Two: Conflict and Rumors of Mutiny

During this stage, group members become preoccupied with dominance, control, and power. The "peer court" is in session. The members try to establish a pecking order. They criticize other members in order to obtain status. There will be a certain degree of hostility toward the leader because the unrealistic expectations of his or her abilities to create change are dashed. The magical aspects of his person are shrinking to life-sized proportions.

Also members feel disillusioned. They sense they will not be rewarded by the leader as the favored member of the group. Some participants will attack the leader and others will rally to defend him or her. Some will doubt the entire process during this stage.

Stage Three: Group Cohesiveness

In this stage the morale of the group improves. There is a sense of cooperation and a desire to unite so that the bonds of intimacy can be built. The group will enjoy a rich experience of self-disclosure. In a sense, they have forgiven the leader for falling from his or her pedestal, and they are ready to see what the group members can offer in terms of support and feedback. Be aware that there is a potential for negative feelings to be suppressed in order to maintain the cohesiveness. The gamut of emotions must be open for expression. The group's hostility must emerge if the group is going to mature. When you cross this barrier, the group will be able to address issues such as style of relating, hatred of God, contempt, and the complexities of bold love.

Stage Four: Termination

The ending of a group is an integral part of the process and should never be overlooked. If closure is handled well, it can be an important force in promoting change. Closure reveals to group members the meaning of continuing to love in spite of the sadness of separation. For some group members, the thought of ending the group is threatening. Their defense against this transition often is to resurrect former issues in order to legitimize their need to stay in the support group.

The group labors mightily to construct a bridge that is durable enough to bear the weight of sadness. Once the bridge is in place, the members must face the sorrow so that it transports them to the task of boldly loving new people. They have a new calling to give away the surplus they have harvested from the group. It is often important for the member who is leaving to talk through his or her decision. The group will feel respected and profit from being included in the decision. It is best if termination is a constructive and affirming statement about the person's progress through the duration of the group.[1]

Group Evaluation

Encourage each member to make an evaluation of the group during the second half of the group experience, after chapter 6 of the workbook. Here are some suggested questions:

1. How do you think the group is contributing to your growth?

2. How is the group hindering your growth?

3. What would you like to see remain the same?

4. What would you like to see change?

5. How close are you feeling to the other group members? What is it like for you to be in these relationships?

6. How distant are you feeling? What is that like?

Termination Activities

Here are several options to choose from to help facilitate healthy termination of the group. Think through the personality of your group, and choose the one that suits it best.

Letter to the Group

Before the last session, each participant writes a letter to be read at the last session of the group. It is written to the group members. Participants write about the things they will take away from the group. What have they learned? What thoughts or feelings do they have about group members? What would they say to someone beginning to face sexual abuse issues? What desires do they have for other group members?

Cards of Encouragement

Each participant writes his or her name on one side of several index cards. During the last group session, these cards are passed around to all other participants. All the members write a sentence or two of appreciation about the person or the hopes they have for the person in the future. The cards are then given to the appropriate members at the end of the meeting.

Regrets

During the final meeting, participants are asked to imagine leaving, getting into their cars, and driving away. They would look in their rear-view mirrors back at the place they are leaving. They try to imagine what they would regret not having said before they left. Then they begin talking through any unfinished business or emotions they have about the group and its members.

Here are some questions to consider addressing during your final session:

- •What are your feelings about ending the group?
- •What do you feel loss and sadness about?
- •What is it like to say goodbye? How have you departed from loved ones in the past? Do you believe this goodbye will be different or the same?
- •How would you long for others to say goodbye to you?

NOTE

1. The stages of a group are adapted from Irvin D. Yalom, *The Theory and Practice of Group Psychotherapy* (New York: Basic Books, 1985).